World University Library

The World University Library is an international
series of books, each of which has been specially
commissioned. The authors are leading scientists
and scholars from all over the world who, in an age
of increasing specialisation, see the need for a
broad, up-to-date presentation of their subject.
The aim is to provide authoritative introductory
books for university students which will be of
interest also to the general reader.
The series is published in Britain, France, Germany,
Holland, Italy, Spain, Sweden and the United States.

Frontispiece. Alexander Pushkin, by Kiprensky (1827).

Ronald Hingley

Russian Writers and Society,

1825–1904

World University Library

McGraw-Hill Book Company
New York   Toronto

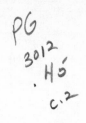

© Ronald Hingley 1967
Library of Congress Catalog Card Number 66–16480
Phototypeset by BAS Printers Limited, Wallop, Hampshire, England
Printed by Officine Grafiche Arnoldo Mondadori, Verona, Italy

Contents

Preface

It is chiefly to the Russian novel and short story of 1825–1904 that the present study supplies a background, though some attention is given to other literary genres – poetry, drama, criticism, memoir-writing and autobiography – in which nineteenth-century Russians also excelled. But to the world at large prose fiction is the supreme Russian literary achievement, besides being an area in which a knowledge of the background can be particularly valuable.

Some readers may feel that the case for such a background study needs arguing, since a Russian novel so often seems to be an exploration of the general human predicament, not an account of individuals in definite places on precise dates. The setting may be identified as Russian – but cautiously, so that many stories and novels take place in 'the village of B', a 'certain' provincial town or 'T— District', as if the authors themselves wanted to keep things as vague as possible, which for various reasons they often did.

Yet Russian writers were at work in a specific society consisting of many millions of diverse and active people, where many different things were going on at the same time. While Turgenev was elaborating the character of his ineffectual and talkative super-fluous man Rudin in his first novel, published in 1856, the Crimean port of Sevastopol was under siege and the Russians had the charge of the Light Brigade made against them by the British army – an episode which did not greatly disturb their *sang-froid*. The year when Goncharov's great, slow-moving novel *Oblomov* appeared (1859) was also the year in which the Caucasian guerrilla chief Shamil surrendered to the Russians in the mountain village of Gunib, while in the far east the Russian governor-general of Siberia was taking over huge areas which the Chinese regarded as their own. While Muscovites were following the progress of Anna Karenin's love affair with Count Vronsky in the pages of *The Russian Herald* in the years 1875–7, the troops of General Michael Skobelev were battering the Central Asiatic Khanate of Kokand into submission nearly two thousand miles away – quite apart from the fact that war with Turkey was brewing up somewhat nearer home. Such distant places and exotic climes often figure in literary works. Even the sedentary Goncharov made a journey round the world, as described in his *Frigate Pallas* (1856). Tolstoy fought in the Caucasus and Crimea, and so extended his range of subject-matter, while Pushkin defied Turkish bullets and the displeasure of Tsar Nicholas I when he attached himself to the Russian army, as described in his *Journey to Erzerum* (1836).

How was imperial Russia administered and how was it attacked from inside by its political enemies? What is a zemstvo and what sort of objects would you expect to find in a peasant's hut? Who wore uniform? Who attended what schools and universities? Who might expect to be 'sent to Siberia' and what would happen to him there? How did Russians travel over their enormous distances? What was the status of a Cossack, a Jew, a Tatar or a Baltic baron? Russian literature and its review of the human predicament would surely gain if readers had more precise conceptions of such things than is sometimes the case.

The present study attempts to answer such questions systematically, and thus to supply readers of a later age and of other nationalities with the kind of background that Russian nineteenth-century authors assumed their readers to possess. Many of the greatest Russian writers wrote only with contemporary Russian readers in mind, and would have been astonished at the world's enthusiastic acceptance of their work since their death. Some deprecated the very idea of Russian literature being read abroad, and they found it hard to imagine a foreigner who would make sense of what they wrote. 'It will be a long time [Dostoyevsky once warned] before people read our [writers] in Europe, and when they do read them it will be a long time before they understand and appreciate them' (*Diary of a Writer*, July–August, 1877). Chekhov said that his *Cherry Orchard* would be a failure in Berlin and Vienna, 'because they haven't got Lopakhins or students *à la* Trofimov' (letter of 4th March 1904). Thus some of the greatest Russian authors wrote as if their readers were already initiated into the mysteries of imperial Russia, and they did not bother

Russia in Europe: administrative boundaries (late nineteenth century).
Where the name of a town is underlined, it is the same name
as the province or region of which it is the capital. Thus <u>Tambov</u>
is the capital of Tambov Province. The administrative areas
are smaller than those of Russia in Asia (see map on pp. 50–51)
because of European Russia's greater population density.

about the untutored foreigner. The aim here is therefore to supply the kind of information which Russian authors often took for granted in their readers. In fact 'Lopakhins' and 'students à la Trofimov' are precisely the kind of topic on which information is given in this book.

An attempt has also been made to evoke the peculiar and fascinating atmosphere of imperial Russia. A foreign scholar would be foolish indeed if he sought to rival the vivid pictures of imperial society painted by Pushkin, Herzen, Tolstoy, Turgenev and so many others. But he can draw on their works for illustration, as has been done here. To a limited extent therefore this brief study supplies a commentary on the more important literary works of the period, but it does not even attempt a systematic review of the rich subject-matter of nineteenth-century Russian literature. Illustrations are mainly taken from the better-known works and authors, and the temptation to unearth little-known curiosities has often had to be resisted for reasons of space.

The intention is to describe and evoke imperial Russia, not to evaluate or criticise it – still less to abuse it, as one is constantly encouraged to do by Soviet Russian tirades against the 'Tsarist régime', a phrase which will not be found in the text below. Cruelty, injustice and exploitation have unhappily been a feature of both pre-1917 and post-1917 Russia, and it is arguable that the similarities between the two outweigh the much-advertised differences. Imperial Russia does have certain attractive features, in that its spokesmen were more modest – less prone than are their Soviet successors to claim Russian society of their day as a sort of ideal popular democracy. And imperial Russians were also less apt to obtrude their political system as a model which the rest of the world should be bullied or cajoled into copying – in fact they tended to speak as if they were rather ashamed of it. On the other hand, the advantages are by no means all on one side.

Although a comparative evaluation of imperial and Soviet Russia forms no part of the subject-matter of the present study, there is a reason why the topic must be mentioned in the preface.

This is that to describe the often unsavoury facts of life of imperial Russia without some qualification is to risk associating oneself by implication with Soviet Russian denunciations of the bad old days. It therefore seems important to stress once more that a comparison between the two societies, admittedly an important topic meriting patient and scholarly consideration, happens not to be a theme of the present study – though occasional parallels are drawn in passing. Old Russia and new Russia are both fascinating subjects, but it is tempting to add that no 'western' person in his senses would ever have chosen to be a citizen of either. In any case, as stated, the aim here has been to describe, not to judge.

Some difficulty has, incidentally, occurred in choosing English tenses to describe the many features of imperial Russia that continue to exist more or less unchanged in Soviet Russia – such things as the climate and the ritual of the Orthodox Church. When such topics are discussed in the past tense, this is not necessarily meant to imply that the situation has changed, but is simply a stylistic convenience. An attempt to be strict in keeping the present tense where appropriate would have led to endless qualifications and reservations without corresponding gain.

The transliteration and handling of Russian names adopted here are as laid down at length on pp. xi–xvi of vol. iii of *The Oxford Chekhov* (London, 1964; New York, 1965), edited by myself. Dates relating to Russia before 1918 are given in the 'old style' – that is, they lag behind the calendar in use in western Europe by twelve days in the nineteenth century and by thirteen days in the twentieth century. References given in the text normally include only the author's name, and for fuller details readers should consult the bibliography, where authors are listed alphabetically within each of the four sections. Translations into English occurring in the text are my own except where otherwise attributed, and mentions of Tolstoy are to be taken as referring to the novelist Leo Tolstoy except where otherwise indicated.

PART ONE

The writer's situation

1 Russian literature from 1825 to 1904

Russian writers were producing original work long before 1825, but without creating any of the world's acknowledged literary masterpieces, and though some eight centuries of earlier development provide rewarding material for the literary scholar, he will look in vain for a Russian Dante, Cervantes, Shakespeare, Molière or Goethe. It was only in the 1820s and with the arrival of Pushkin that Russian literature first began to take its place as an important part of European culture.

By 1825 Pushkin was in his middle twenties and well established as a poet. 1825 is also the year in which Chapter One of his novel in verse *Eugene Onegin*, the first important Russian novel as well as one of the greatest, was first published as a whole. The importance of the Russian novel as a genre and the superiority of Pushkin, for Russians, over all their other writers, combine to make 1825 the start of the great age. And, as the beginning of Nicholas I's reign, coinciding with the suppression of the Decembrist revolt, it is a historical landmark too.

1904, the year of Chekhov's death, provides a neat finish to the period. As a master of prose fiction and dramatist, Chekhov was one of the titans, and no Russian writer of comparable status has arisen since. Conveniently for literary historians, his death occurred on the eve of another turning-point in Russian history, the revolution of 1905. Thus the great age of Russian literature ended as it had begun, with an attempt to overthrow the autocracy. Russian literature did not die with Chekhov any more than it had been born with Pushkin, but Chekhov was the last in the line of the Russian classics which had begun with Pushkin and continued through Lermontov, Turgenev, Goncharov and Tolstoy.

The age of the novel

Within the eighty years 1825–1904 a core of two and a half decades forms the peak period for the Russian novel, starting with Turgenev's *Rudin* (1856) and ending with Dostoyevsky's *Brothers Karamazov* (1879–80). This bracket includes Tolstoy's two most important novels (*War and Peace*, 1865–9; *Anna Karenin*, 1875–7) and Dostoyevsky's four masterpieces (*Crime and Punishment*, 1866; *The Idiot*, 1868–9; *Devils*, 1871–2 – also known in translation as *The Possessed* – as well as *The Brothers Karamazov*). It also includes Goncharov's *Oblomov* and all six of Turgenev's novels (*Rudin*, followed by *A Nest of Gentlefolk*, 1859; *On the Eve*, 1860; *Fathers and Children*, 1862; *Smoke*, 1867; *Virgin Soil*, 1877). Turgenev's six novels are a formidable body of work taken as a whole, even though some are weaker than others and their total length is less than half that of *War and Peace*.

Thus the great age of the novel coincides with the reign of a single Tsar, Alexander II, from 1855 to 1881 – once more as if literature and history had conspired to make a tidy pattern. Many other novels came out in Alexander II's reign as well as those mentioned above. They include Pisemsky's *A Thousand Souls* (1858), Goncharov's *Precipice* (1869), Leskov's *Cathedral Folk* (1872) and Saltykov-Shchedrin's *Golovlyov Family* (1876–80). But none of these can challenge comparison with the thirteen titles listed above. Nor, probably, can any novel written after Alexander II's reign Tolstoy's *Resurrection* (1899), Sologrub's *Little Devil* (1907), Bely's *Petersburg* (1913), Sholokhov's *Quiet Don* (1928–40) and Pasternak's *Doctor Zhivago* (1958) are all remarkable works, while *Foma Gordeyev* (1899), *The Artamonovs' Business* (1925) and others of Gorky's novels have their admirers. But rightly or wrongly none of these works enjoys the distinction of the thirteen titles mentioned in the previous paragraph.

These thirteen titles meet more severe competition from three

The hanged Decembrists – sketches made by Pushkin on the margin of a manuscript. The Decembrist rising, which took place in St Petersburg on 14 December 1825, was the first revolutionary action against the imperial autocracy. The rising was easily put down, five leaders were hanged and many of the conspirators were sent to Siberia. Pushkin was a friend of many of the Decembrists and their fate was a severe personal blow to him.

especially important earlier works which bring the total of leading Russian novels to sixteen. These are Pushkin's *Eugene Onegin* (1825–31), Lermontov's *Hero of Our Time* (1839–40) and Gogol's *Dead Souls*, Part One (1842). All of them have claims to be considered the greatest Russian novel, and all influenced later writing. As these pioneer works suggest, the Russian novel sprang in a sense out of poetry, for the three authors include the greatest Russian poet in Pushkin and another leading poet in Lermontov. Gogol was not a poet, such verse as he wrote being ephemeral, but it may be mentioned that novels were commonly called poems at the time, and *Dead Souls* is so described on its title page.

Realist fiction

Literatures often blossom in verse before they flower in prose, and Russian literature was no exception. The 1820s were the golden age of Russian poetry, that of Pushkin and his contemporaries, while the 1830s were the heyday of romantic poetry as represented by Lermontov and Tyutchev (though Tyutchev continued to write until the 1870s). But it was not until the 1840s that an important movement – as opposed to important individual authors – could be discerned in Russian prose.

This was not for want of looking. Belinsky, who remains the foremost name in Russian criticism, was so keenly on the watch for a great period in Russian literature that he was proclaiming its arrival while it was still barely in sight. He used the term 'natural school' to describe what seemed to him the most significant current in Russian prose writing of the 1840s. Prose literature of the time seemed to be evolving under Gogol's influence, which in the end proved less potent than was anticipated. After sensing the first stirrings of the coming great age of Russian prose, Belinsky died in 1848, too early to see his natural school evolve away from Gogol into Russian realism.

It is arguable that realism and realist, used as descriptive terms, are misleading if applied to the dominant strain among Russian

Left. Vissarion Belinsky (1811–48), the most famous Russian literary critic of the nineteenth century and a pioneer of Russian radicalism.
Right. Nicholas Leskov (1831–95), the leading 'sociological' fiction-writer of the century.
Far right. Aleksey Pisemsky (1820–81), novelist and playwright.

writings of the second half of the nineteenth century, but it is rather late to say so now because these terms acquired currency long ago. 'Realism' will be used here mainly as a label, and it is hoped that it will be regarded more as the brand name on a varied set of bottles than as a description of contents.

The Russian realist school may be regarded as beginning in the late 1840s. The years 1846–7 show an explosion of talent, less in the quality of work produced than in the number of new writers who then published their first immature work and later achieved fame with more lasting contributions. It was in these years that three leading realist novelists mentioned above made their début: Dostoyevsky with his short novels *Poor Folk* and *The Double* (both 1846), Turgenev with *Khor and Kalinych* (1847) – the first of his *Sportsman's Sketches*, published as a whole in 1852 – and Goncharov with his novel *A Common Story* (1847). Though Tolstoy became known somewhat later (readers had to wait until 1852 for his first publication, *Childhood*), other important realists also brought out their first work in the late 1840s, including Ostrovsky with scenes from his play *All in the Family* (1847). D. V. Grigorovich began publishing in 1844 and brought out *The Village* and *Poor Anton* in 1846 and 1847 – two stories which proved influential because of the emphasis put on the miseries of peasant life. Pisemsky's first published work also belongs to this period, as does that of Herzen, including his novel *Whose Fault?* (1845–6). And it was in 1846 that Nekrasov bought the review *The Contemporary*

(St Petersburg, 1836–66), which became for twenty years the most influential Russian literary monthly and the main vehicle for the emerging realist movement.

Thus Russian realism was launched in the late 1840s, and ten years later it was producing masterpieces. Of these the thirteen novels from *Rudin* to *The Brothers Karamazov*, mentioned above, are the supreme achievement, but form only a small part of the achievements of Russian realism. To them may be added many minor works by the four novelists concerned (Turgenev, Tolstoy, Dostoyevsky and Goncharov) as well as the writings of Pisemsky, Leskov, S. T. Aksakov, Ostrovsky and others.

Though realism has been deprecated as a descriptive term, being used more as a label, certain characteristics do loosely unite the Russian writers to whom the term is commonly applied. These include a preference for portraying Russian life contemporary with the author in a Russian setting; a straightforward, plain, functional style; and a tendency to include detailed factual description of such things as landscape, dress and physical appearance.

Not all works termed realist fully conform with these qualifications. Thus *War and Peace* does not portray contemporary Russian life, being a historical novel set more than half a century before the period in which it was written. Aksakov's *Family Chronicle* (1856) and *The Childhood of Bagrov the Grandson* (1858) are also set in the past, and draw, like *War and Peace*, on the author's own family history. Turgenev's *Smoke* is not placed in

Fyodor Dostoyevsky (1821–81), by V. Perov, painted in 1872. Dostoyevsky was a radical in youth and was sentenced to execution on a charge of conspiracy – a sentence commuted at the last moment to gaol and exile to Siberia. Later he returned to St Petersburg and became a pillar of reaction.

Russia, but in Baden-Baden. Then again, no one could call the style of Dostoyevsky's earliest fiction plain, modelled as it is on that of the exuberantly tortuous Gogol. Nor is detailed factual description by any means always the rule. Tolstoy's later 'popular' stories convey simple morals to simple people in spare language, while Chekhov's descriptions are so economical that they make some of his predecessors seem lush by comparison. Still, by and large the characteristics given above are valid for the Russian realists.

Others which are sometimes advanced apply less fully. When critics claim neglect of plot in favour of characterisation as a feature of the school, one wonders whether they are being misled by the leisurely pace of some Russian realists. A plot may be slow-moving, as in Goncharov's *Oblomov*, yet effective. Some realist works – *Crime and Punishment* and *Anna Karenin* – are triumphs of plot construction, and even Chekhov's stories often have more plot than is sometimes conceded to them.

Another quality claimed for the realist school is human sympathy. 'People are not good or bad, they are only more or less unhappy and deserving of sympathy – this may be taken as the formula of all the Russian novelists from Turgenev to Chekhov' (Mirsky, pp. 170–1). True, Goncharov, Turgenev and Tolstoy do bear out this claim. But what of Dostoyevsky's monumental villains? What of Saltykov-Shchedrin's monstrous *Golovlyov Family*? Or of the ogres of insensitivity and selfishness in the work of Chekhov himself?

Are these works realist in being 'true to life', to mention a cliché which often comes up in such discussions? It is not always clear just what those who use the phrase understand by 'life', which can mean different things to different people, as the evidence of literature confirms. One of the attractions of literature, in fact, is that each author recreates life according to his personal vision of it. And even if 'truth to life' could be accepted as a criterion, it would apply only partially to the Russian realists. Gogol himself has sometimes been claimed as a realist and even as the father of

Russian realism, though admittedly this view is hard to sustain. But Gogol was a caricaturist and dealt in exaggeration. That a man should wake up one day to find his nose missing and should later notice it going about disguised as a senior civil servant – this typical episode from his story *The Nose* (1835) hardly conforms to the average man's experience of life. Nor have most people had private interviews with the devil, as happens to one of Dostoyevsky's heroes, Ivan Karamazov. And even in nineteenth-century Russia, prostitutes, epileptics, suicides, murderers, lunatics and torturers were not so thick on the ground as Dostoyevsky's works suggest. Is Turgenev's treatment of love realist? Or is it, at least in the vulgar sense of the word, romantic? Even Chekhov, apparently truest to life of all, is suspect. Surely relationships between men and women are not so uniformly frustrating as is indicated in his pages – any more than they are always as sentimental and Wertheresque as Turgenev tends to imply. The less said about truth to life the better.

Perhaps the most important quality of the great Russian realists, and one which more than any other unites them, is a certain common attitude to themselves and their world – an agreement on the importance of being, in the best sense of the word, earnest. They were serious about man and man's destiny in a new and characteristically Russian way. Some held strong views and wanted to put them over, while others were less dogmatic, but meant at least to formulate the riddles of Russian life and human existence even if they could not solve them. This seriousness is surely one of the reasons why Russian nineteenth-century literature has caught the imagination of the world – especially as some writers, including Gogol, Dostoyevsky and Chekhov, combine it with humour of a special Russian brand. But humorous or not, the Russian realist author usually felt himself to be more than a mere entertainer.

The Russian novel lost impetus at the end of the 1870s. 1881, the year of Alexander II's assassination, was also that of Dostoyevsky's death. Turgenev died two years later, and Tolstoy, who was to live on until 1910, died a sort of literary death in the late seventies at the time of his conversion to his own brand of Christianity. He was never to repeat the triumph of *Anna Karenin* and almost turned his back on fiction as he had hitherto practised it in order to become a moralist. Goncharov too was a spent force long before his death in 1891.

Chekhov and the drama

Thus the age of the giants was over by 1880, when Chekhov published his first writings. During the next twenty-five years he stood well above all other still-living Russian writers of prose fiction except for Tolstoy, whose main achievements were in the past. Chekhov was not a novelist, since his only attempt at a novel, *The Shooting Party* (1884), is a lightweight effort. He began his literary career as the writer of facetious sketches about such things as funny mothers-in-law, but had found his level by 1888 as an original short-story writer. The fifty-eight stories written between the beginning of that year and his death give him a special position in Russian literature, and the importance of this corpus is arguably even greater than that of *War and Peace* or *The Brothers Karamazov*. No other Russian except Gogol, Tolstoy and Leskov, whose methods were different, is worth mentioning in the same breath as a short-story writer. But many readers would go further and claim Chekhov as the greatest Russian writer of all.

Chekhov also became Russia's greatest dramatist, though on his home territory Ostrovsky with his larger dramatic *oeuvre* is a more serious rival than he seems to foreigners. Otherwise Russian drama of the period can most simply be regarded as a series of brilliant individual efforts by authors who have all written other dramatic work, but are remembered by most theatre-goers for one play only: Griboyedov for *Woe from Wit* (written in 1822–4); Gogol for *The Inspector General* (1836); Turgenev for *A Month in the Country* (1850); Tolstoy for *The Power of Darkness* (1888) and Gorky for *The Lower Depths* (1902).

БЫЛОЕ И ДУМЫ

ИСКЕНДЕРА.

ТОМЪ ТРЕТIЙ

ЛОНДОНЪ
TRÜBNER & Co., PATERNOSTER ROW.
1861.

Memoirs

A few examples of autobiographies and collections of memoirs must also be mentioned, among which Herzen's *My Past and Thoughts* (1852–68) is outstanding. It is often used below to illustrate aspects of Nicholas I's Russia, and its value is enhanced by the fact that it was not subject to Russian censorship, having been produced abroad. Gorky's story of his early life, often considered his most important work, covers the period considered here, though it was written and published later, in three parts: *Childhood* (1913–14); *In the World* (1915–16) and *My Universities* (1923). To this must be added the same author's *Reminiscences* (1924–31) of writers who include Chekhov and Tolstoy.

Thinly disguised autobiographies or family reminiscences – written to a great extent about the author himself and his own family, but preserving the outward form of fiction – also occupy an honoured place in nineteenth-century Russian literature. The genre includes Aksakov's reminiscences and studies of family history going back into the eighteenth century, of which his *Family Chronicle* and *Childhood of Bagrov the Grandson* were mentioned above. It also includes Dostoyevsky's *Notes from the House of the*

Dead (1862); and Tolstoy's trilogy, *Childhood* (1852), *Boyhood* (1854) and *Youth* (1857). These works all provide valuable evidence on the authors themselves in specific Russian social contexts, even if the main characters bear the names 'Bagrov', 'Goryanchikov' and 'Irtenyev' rather than their real names – Aksakov, Dostoyevsky and Tolstoy respectively.

Poetry

This brief sketch of Russian literature of the great age must be ended with some further reference to poetry. After the blossoming of Pushkin, Lermontov and other poets of the 1820s and 1830s, verse yielded first place to prose until the end of the century, but by no means disappeared from the scene. In mid-century it was sustained by Nekrasov's writings, often propagandist in intent, but original and memorable, his longest and most important work being *Who Can Be Happy in Russia?* (1873–6). Nekrasov proclaimed himself obsessed with his duties as a citizen to lighten the lot of his fellow-Russians, especially the downtrodden peasantry. Among other mid-century poets Tyutchev, who continued to write, Afanasy Fet and Apollon Maykov, were less civic-minded than Nekrasov and more concerned to create works of art. At the turn of the century the desire to rise above Russian writers' traditional preoccupations with their civic duty contributed to the philosophy of the symbolist movement in Russian poetry, of which Blok was the most prominent representative.

2 The writer's life and mission

Social position

Many Russian nineteenth-century writers belonged, particularly in the first part of the period, to the Russian gentry, that is to the upper classes. Many also belonged to an élite within the gentry, the class of country landowners, from which Pushkin, Turgenev and Tolstoy sprang. These writers came from families which had been supported for generations by serf labour, an influence illustrated as potentially demoralising by another member of the group, Goncharov, in his novel *Oblomov*.

Membership of the gentry was not necessarily a sign of exalted social origin. Dostoyevsky too belonged to it, but was resentful of such social superiors as Turgenev and Tolstoy. Dostoyevsky's father was an army doctor who retired from the service to practise as a civilian before Dostoyevsky was born and in course of time decided to add to the status of gentleman, which he possessed in law, the additional cachet of rural landowner. He bought two villages complete, since this was in the days of serfdom, with their inhabitants. A few years later he was murdered by his own serfs, something that occasionally happened even in the best regulated Russian county families.

In the course of the century literature and cultural life were more and more opened to persons of humble social origin known as *raznochintsy*, of which 'other ranks' is a rough English translation. Belinsky, son of a poor doctor, was one of these, and so were Chernyshevsky and Dobrolyubov who belonged to the most characteristic group of the *raznochintsy*, that of the seminarists (pupils of seminaries for the sons of priests). Chekhov was a grocer's son and Gorky, another social upstart, came of a poor family and worked in his youth as a shop-boy, baker, washer-up on a Volga steamship and so on, thus graduating as the first major writer closely associated with the Russian proletariat. From the largest and most humble social class, the peasantry, literature had few recruits.

Nicholas Dobrolyubov (1836–61).
Lithograph by Borel, 1861.
Dobrolyubov was a prominent literary and social critic. He was for
several years the chief critic on
Russia's most important radical
journal, *The Contemporary*. His character and early death caused him to be
regarded as a sort of saintly martyr of
Russian radicalism. But he was not in
fact persecuted by the authorities,
except through the medium of censorship, and he died a natural death.

Hazards of authorship

Having considered how certain Russian writers were born, one
may also profitably note how some of them died, since this makes
it easier to understand a Russian's attitude to his literature. There
is a tendency for modern readers to look on writers of the last
century as sedentary creatures musing gently at their desks, and
this impression seems to be borne out by the leisurely pace of
Russian novels, so often set in the dreamy world of country
estates where life flows on through several hundred pages of print
without much happening. In fact, however, most nineteenth-
century Russian writers were not typically Victorian or Trollopian
figures. How could they be in an age and country where life and
liberty were so precarious?

Two leading poets were killed in duels: Pushkin at the age of
thirty-seven and Lermontov at twenty-seven. Both had already
been exiled – Pushkin for showing leanings towards atheism in a
private letter picked up by the authorities, Lermontov for blaming
Pushkin's death on the imperial Establishment in his *Death of a
Poet* (circulated in 1837). Both poets felt themselves persecuted by
authority, and Lermontov at least was the kind of person to derive
perverse satisfaction from this – but not Pushkin, who especially
resented the authorities' refusal to let him travel abroad. After

1826, when he was released from exile, interviewed by Nicholas I and placed under the Tsar's personal protection, he still felt crushed by the weight of imperial patronage, exercised through Nicholas's chief of gendarmes, Count Benckendorff.

Many of Pushkin's contemporaries were punished for their part in the Decembrist revolt of 1825. Several were poets: Kondraty Ryleyev (one of the five leaders who were hanged), Alexander Odoyevsky and Wilhelm Küchelbecker (who were exiled to Siberia). Another writer and friend of Pushkin's, the romantic novelist and poet Alexander Bestuzhev, who wrote under the pseudonym Marlinsky, was sentenced to twenty years' hard labour, later commuted to service in the Caucasus as a private soldier, for his part in the uprising.

A combination of these misfortunes overtook Dostoyevsky. Sentenced in 1849 to execution for his association with a political discussion group, he was led out with a number of others to be shot – a sadistic joke staged on the direct orders of Nicholas I. After some of the victims had been clothed in shrouds by soldiers, an especially grisly detail, commutation of the sentence was announced at the last possible moment, by previous arrangement. Dostoyevsky had to spend some ten years in Siberia, four as a convict in the gaol at Omsk, and the rest as a private and officer in a Siberian army unit.

In a way Dostoyevsky had asked for trouble. But even Turgenev,

Far left. The poet Kondraty Ryleyev (1795–1826), one of
the five Decembrists who were hanged. (Pastel by
Mikhaylovsky.)
Left. Wilhelm Küchelbecker (1797–1846), as sketched by
his friend, fellow-poet and one-time schoolmate, Pushkin.
Küchelbecker was imprisoned and exiled for his part in the
Decembrist rising of 1825.

altogether more cautious, did not escape the imperial police. His
punishment was milder, since he was only kept under arrest for a
month in 1852 and then exiled to his country estate for sixteen
months. The reason for this was deliciously Russian: he had
indiscreetly written an obituary of Gogol, published in Moscow at
a time when articles on Gogol were prohibited in the St Petersburg
press. As this reminds one, the authorities usually became nervous
whenever a writer died because of a Russian tradition of making
the obsequies of a leading author the occasion for political demonstrations. Over thirty years later Turgenev's own death proved no
exception (see p. 144). He would, incidentally, have died a lot
sooner if Tolstoy had had his way. A bitter quarrel between the
two writers came to a head in 1861, when Turgenev insulted
Tolstoy, who challenged him to a duel on most unusual terms,
since it was to be fought with rifles and, apparently, without
seconds. Fortunately this unhappy event did not take place, as
otherwise the world might have been robbed of *Smoke*, *Virgin Soil*,
War and Peace, *Anna Karenin* and much else.

The tally of distinguished exiles was a large one. In addition to
some already mentioned, Herzen was banished to Perm, Vyatka
(now Kirov), Vladimir and Novgorod at various times before
leaving Russia for ever in 1847. The radical critic and political
thinker Chernyshevsky is one of the many literary figures who
suffered more severely. He spent more than half his adult life in
prison and exile, mainly in remote parts of Siberia, and his resolute
defiance of authority makes him one of the most illustrious
political prisoners. The short-story writer Korolenko was exiled
to Siberia (from 1879 to 1885) and was not permitted to live in St
Petersburg until 1895. Many other writers also met lurid fates –
the short-story writer Garshin, who commited suicide in 1888,
the radical publicist Pisarev, who drowned in 1868, and the
playwright-diplomat Griboyedov, who was torn to pieces by
a Persian mob in 1829. Others became more or less deranged
(Gogol, Goncharov), or were officially declared so in defiance
of the facts (Chaadayev).

Count Tolstoy and his wife photographed in 1910, the year of his death. This is the last photograph to have been taken of Tolstoy. The declining decades of this celebrated married couple were marred by quarrels and misunderstandings which arose from disputes over money and the Countess's refusal to behave as a Tolstoyan simple-lifer.

Still, there were some who contrived to die from natural causes, not directly assisted by authority. Tuberculosis, the great nineteenth-century killer, claimed two important victims: Belinsky at the age of thirty-six and Chekhov at the age of forty-four. But the rugged Tolstoy survived until his ninth decade. Like Pasternak later, he was protected by international fame from the persecution that he seemed to challenge, and suffered only the ludicrous fate of being excommunicated by the Russian Orthodox Church in 1901, on which occasion he 'positively refused to accept congratulations'. But even Tolstoy hastened his end by running away from home at the age of eighty-two.

Writing for a living

Nineteenth-century Russian writers were concerned with the human condition and with problems of philosophy, religion or ethics and, as befits the high-minded, were often financially incompetent. But this does not mean that they never thought about money. They lived in the everyday world as well as in the world of the imagination, and there were times when most of them were aware that they and their families had to be fed and housed.

The main nineteenth-century Russian writers were all professional authors, depending at least in part on the earnings of their pens. Even Pushkin, very much a member of the élite, could point the contrast with an earlier age when he said, 'I am not one of our eighteenth-century writers', and explained that, though he wrote for himself, he published for money (letter of 8th March 1824). He also said that he looked on his finished poems 'as a cobbler looks on a pair of his boots. I sell for profit' (letter of March [undated] 1823). Prevented by the Tsar from publishing *Boris Godunov* (written in 1825), Pushkin told Benckendorff that for him to be deprived of some 15,000 roubles which his tragedy might bring him – would be an 'inconvenience' (letter of 7th January 1830). This was a masterly understatement, because Pushkin was in fact very angry.

Anton Chekhov, with his family and friends in 1890 in front of their home on Sadovo-Kudrinskaya Street in Moscow in 1890. *Top row, left to right*: Ivan and Alexander (brothers), Paul (father). *Second row*: unknown, Lika Mizinov, Masha (sister), Mother, Seryozha Kiselev. *Bottom row*: Misha (brother), Anton.

Other authors from the gentry such as Tolstoy and Turgenev were also anxious to earn money from their writings. True, Tolstoy infuriated his wife by renouncing, in 1891, the copyright of all his works written after *Anna Karenin* and thus ceasing to receive royalties. He had in effect taken a vow of poverty, but Countess Tolstoy certainly had not, and retained control over his copyrights up to and including *Anna Karenin*. The Tolstoys could afford the luxury of such manoeuvres, but as a younger man Tolstoy had behaved more conventionally. His short novel *Cossacks* (1863) might never have been published at all if he had not lost a large sum of money at cards and been compelled to accept an advance against the uncompleted and abandoned novel from the publisher of the monthly *Russian Herald*, M. N. Katkov.

Such episodes were part of the fabric of Dostoyevsky's life. He was sometimes forced to pawn his trousers and underclothes, and was for many years a compulsive gambler. Few authors have signed a literary contract more absurd than that for the short novel *The Gambler*, which bound him to a publishing shark called Stellovsky. The agreement contained penalty clauses stopping just short of hard labour for life. But this affair had a happy ending: Dostoyevsky hurriedly engaged a girl who could take shorthand, did a rush job on the novel (but wrote a minor masterpiece), fulfilled his contract and married his stenographer – not bad for a few weeks' work.

Chekhov took up writing because he needed money, having become chief provider for a large family in his early twenties. In those days he often had to hang round editorial offices to get his fee, and editors would try to fob him off with payment in kind. One indulgently told him to 'go along to my tailor's and order yourself a pair of trousers'. Or theatre tickets might be offered in place of cash. In 1899 Chekhov, now an established writer, sold the copyright of all his published work except drama to the publisher A. F. Marks by a contract which turned out a bad bargain. Like most Russian nineteenth-century authors, he could have done with a good literary agent, for there were plenty of Stellovskys about.

Thus the biographies and correspondence of Russian nineteenth-century authors contain more references to hard cash than to the Russian soul. Writers were constantly fussing about money, and yet were grotesquely easy-going in their financial arrangements. Loans were readily granted, gambled away or forgotten by the debtor. Frenzied appeals, orgies of self-justification, quarrels and reconciliations were the usual accompaniment to these transactions. A famous literary quarrel, that between Turgenev and Dostoyevsky, shows a leading westernist and slavophile locked in conflict over principles, but it is tempting to see the real bone of contention in the fifty thalers lent by Turgenev to Dostoyevsky in 1865. Dostoyevsky offered to repay the money in three weeks, but took ten years. Turgenev might forgive him, but that was not the point. Dostoyevsky could not forgive Turgenev for doing him the favour in the first place.

Where established authors were involved, an advance would often have been paid and spent before serious work had even begun – a habit which was, of course, by no means confined to the writers of Russia. For periodical publication authors were usually paid by quantity at so many roubles a printer's page (equivalent to about sixteen pages of a book) in the case of longer works, and so much a line for shorter items. So the cynic has an explanation for the excessive length, as is sometimes felt, of the typical Russian novel. After periodical publication the author was usually free to republish in book form as a separate item or as part of a collected edition.

Were Russian authors well paid? They do not seem to have thought so – what author ever does? But established writers were naturally able to obtain special rates. Dostoyevsky caught on comparatively late with the public and often envied Turgenev and Tolstoy, who at one time commanded many more roubles per printer's page than he could hope for. What seemed unfair to Dostoyevsky was that these two authors did not need the money as badly as a literary proletarian, which is what he sometimes called himself.

Serialisation

It was in the periodical press, not in book form, that the bulk of nineteenth-century Russian literature first appeared, which is true of most Russian and Soviet Russian literature down to the present day. Thus each of the sixteen leading Russian novels referred to on p. 15 above, first saw the light of day in a periodical, except for Gogol's *Dead Souls* and with certain qualifications about Pushkin's *Eugene Onegin* (see Pushkin, *Eugene Onegin*, ed. Nabokov, i, pp. 74–83; for further information on periodicals, see also pp. 221–5 below.)

Periodical publication meant that nearly all Russian novels were first brought out as serials, as were those of many leading French and English novelists of the period, including Balzac and Dickens. So it was possible for a large part of a nineteenth-century novel, whether Russian, French or English, to be in print when the ending was little more than a gleam in the author's eye. Thus Tolstoy's *War and Peace* began to appear in the monthly *Russian Herald* in January and February 1865 under the title *1805*. A second batch entitled *War* came out in the same review in February, March and April 1866. At this stage Tolstoy planned a happy ending. The third and final instalment was to be called *All's Well that Ends Well* and in it Prince Andrew's life was to be preserved (Christian, pp. 5–7). This is an instance where an author did not maintain the serial publication of a novel. *War and Peace* continued to roll majestically on, but the rest of it was first published in book form.

Dostoyevsky was also used to seeing large batches of his novels in print long before the endings had been written, but does not seem to have been much put out by one disadvantage of the method – that early chapters of a book commit an author so that he is no longer free to revise his overall plan. For someone so apparently disorganised, Dostoyevsky had a surprisingly clear idea of the future development of his unfinished novels, as his published *Notebooks* show. He claimed that he never accepted an advance from a publisher for what he called a blank space: 'When I've

Nicholas Gogol (1809–52), author of *Dead Souls*, *The Inspector-General* and many superb short stories, including *The Greatcoat*. His writings give an exuberant account of grotesque Russian landowners and officials, but it was not Gogol's intention to write political satire. He was an extreme reactionary and supporter of the imperial autocracy. (Painting by J. F. Moller, 1841.)

received money in advance I have always sold something existing, i.e. I've only sold myself at a point when the poetic idea has already been born and has ripened as far as possible. I have not taken money in advance *for a blank space*, i.e. in the hope of *thinking up* and *composing* a novel by a given date' (see Hingley, *The Undiscovered Dostoyevsky*, p. 108).

'Commitment'

As some of their misfortunes suggest, many Russian writers were hardly pillars of church and state. They tended to be in political opposition, with exceptions such as the ultra-conservative Gogol, and also Dostoyevsky after his return from Siberian exile. But even they were scarcely part of the imperial Establishment. They supported it, each in his eccentric way, but hardly belonged to it. And Gogol's name, through no wish of his own and owing to the construction put on his work by radicals, became a rallying point for political opposition, as the punishment awarded to Turgenev for his obituary notice illustrates.

Radicals or reactionaries, Russian writers did tend to be politically engaged. Many had a crusading fervour, and they had political, ethical, religious, moral or philosophical lessons to teach. In a country lacking free political institutions, literature was a lot better than nothing, hampered though it was by censorship, since it offered some scope even at the worst times for airing political and social opinions. Hence the Russian tradition of looking on the writer as a sage who might perhaps solve the riddle of existence and who was permanently engaged in a 'search for truth', to quote a formula all too often brought up when Russians discuss the writer's role.

Many Russian writers did indeed feel themselves to be in touch with ultimate truth. An extreme case is Gogol, whose great novel *Dead Souls* Part One – was planned as the first instalment of a trilogy designed to regenerate Russia. Parts Two and Three were to be increasingly edifying and to supply the purgatorio and

paradiso to the inferno of Part One, but Gogol's genius was for
describing the squalid and absurd, and so only a fragment of Part
Two and none of Part Three saw the light of day. Unable to portray
virtuous characters convincingly in fiction, he proceeded to address
the nation with sermons on conduct disguised as letters. This
strange document, *Selected Passages from a Correspondence with
Friends* (1847), stung Belinsky to fury, and he denounced Gogol in
an open letter as 'prophet of the knout [Gogol advocated the
flogging of serfs], apostle of ignorance, champion of obscurantism
and panegyrist of Tatar manners'.

Dostoyevsky's views were in some ways a diluted version of

Gogol's, though moderation is hardly a quality which can be associated with Dostoyevsky, who was also well and truly committed. Where Gogol wrote his *Selected Passages*, Dostoyevsky produced his great series of harangues, *The Diary of a Writer* (1873–81). In his novels too Dostoyevsky preached an ideology involving Russia's central role in world history and an original philosophy of good and evil.

Tolstoy was another propagandist and teacher. As is the general human lot, he found this tendency growing stronger as he became older. In *War and Peace* he had been content to develop a comparatively academic philosophy of history, but later came down to a more practical level and tried for instance to stop his readers smoking cigarettes and fornicating, and even to discourage them from reading much of his own fiction. He also inspired a movement based on the ethic of practical Christianity as interpreted by him and including the principle of non-violence.

Gogol, Dostoyevsky and Tolstoy cannot really be called seekers for truth because they had already found it, at least in later life. Other writers were less committed to a doctrine, but still accepted the social command to some extent, feeling obliged to handle political and social themes more wholeheartedly than was the case with most French or English contemporaries. In this Dickens, with his sense of social obligation, stood closer to his Russian colleagues than did many other western writers.

Turgenev was one who adopted the spectator's role rather than that of active participant. His novels span the reign of Alexander II and comment on several important social issues of the period. Thus *Rudin* presents the problem of the 'superfluous man' or odd-man-out, a typical figure in Russian society already described by Pushkin, Lermontov and others; *A Nest of Gentlefolk* shows old-fashioned Russian country life and the pressures of European influence; *On the Eve* looks at the problem of the man of action, which exercised many other Russian writers too; *Fathers and Children* describes the clash between the idealists of the 1840s and the radicals of the 1860s, while *Smoke* treats the conflict between

westernists and slavophiles (see pp. 235–7), and *Virgin Soil* describes the populist movement (see pp. 242–4). Thus Turgenev might have been designed by nature to provide essay subjects for students of nineteenth-century Russian social history. He did hold political and social views, being a moderate liberal and westernist, an opponent of serfdom and so on, but his approach to social problems was more open-minded than many people liked.

So too was Chekhov's. As many comments in his letters show, he resented the tradition according to which Russian writers were pestered by critics and busybodies, and more or less ordered to mobilise themselves on behalf of political and social causes. He hated preaching or being preached at, but did take his role as social observer seriously. He illustrated such problems as the decline of the landowners, the effects of following Tolstoy's teaching in everyday life and the rise of Russian industry. On the thorny problem of the Russian peasant his contributions were superbly eloquent in his characteristically quiet tone.

There were also many writers and critics with extreme left-wing views which they put forward as and when they could. Later developments make this school seem the most influential of all. In a sense it has turned out to be on the winning side, though the claims of the present-day Communist Party of the Soviet Union to be the direct heir of Herzen and Chernyshevsky should not be accepted uncritically. Among radicals and socialists Herzen and Gorky have produced the outstanding autobiographies mentioned above, but on the whole members of this group did not quite belong to the front rank of imaginative writers. Nekrasov and Gorky are the leading creative writers among them, but the bulk of Gorky's work falls outside the period studied here, and he lived on to become the patron saint of Soviet literature.

The radical strain was more dominant in criticism than on the creative side. Even in criticism it did not have a monopoly, but the greatest of all Russian critics, Belinsky, belonged to it, as did his successors, Chernyshevsky and Dobrolyubov. One striking feature of much Russian criticism from Belinsky onwards is the tendency to ignore the literary values and methods of a work of art and to quarry literary works for texts to political and social sermons.

PART TWO

The Empire

Overleaf. Monument on the border of European and Asiatic Russia. The frontier between Europe and Asia provided many a moment of heartbreak for prisoners and exiles under escort to Siberia.

Below. The rooks have arrived; a painting by A. K. Savrasov, 1810. Spring comes on very rapidly in Russia. It is associated with mud, slush, bird-song, colours, smells and ice breaking up on the rivers like an artillery barrage.

3 Geography

Frontiers

By the end of the nineteenth century the boundaries of the Russian Empire enclosed roughly the same huge area as that of its successor state the USSR. The differences were greatest on the western frontiers where Finland and Poland were both part of the territory ruled by the Tsar, Finland enjoying a large measure of autonomy, whereas Poland was a subject nation, especially after 1863. From 1815 to the end of the century Russia's western frontiers remained nearly stable, but in the south and east conditions were fluid, and vast new areas were added to the growing Empire.

Most of the Caucasus, including Transcaucasia, came under Russian rule by submission or conquest between 1801 and 1829. This applies to most of Georgia; to Armenia except for the part which remained to Turkey; and to Azerbaydzhan. The mountaineers of the central Caucasus still resisted in their craggy fortresses, not being completely pacified even with the surrender of their leader Shamil in 1859 and the completed annexation of Circassia in 1864.

The next scene of large-scale expansion was the far east of Siberia. For nearly two centuries the frontier with China had remained as fixed in 1689 by the Treaty of Nerchinsk, but now two new treaties were imposed on the Chinese by N. N. Muravyov, Russian governor-general of Eastern Siberia. By these the Chinese ceded two areas in 1858 and 1860: the left bank of the River Amur and the Maritime Province on the Sea of Japan down to the port of Vladivostok, founded in 1860. The end of the century saw a further important but short-lived strategic gain when the Russians set up their naval base at Port Arthur – acquired on lease from China in 1898, but lost to the Japanese in the Russo–Japanese War of 1904–5. As this shows, the territory of the Empire could contract as well as expand. An earlier, voluntary, instance of this had taken place in 1867 when Russia sold Alaska to the United States for eight million dollars.

Central Asia followed the far east as the chief arena of expansion,

Imperial Russia in the Nineteenth Century, showing the main rivers, lakes, seas, mountains, towns and cities. From the western frontier to the River Yenisey in Central Siberia the greater part of the Empire consisted of a vast plain. To the south and east the frontiers almost everywhere coincided with mountains, rivers or seas.

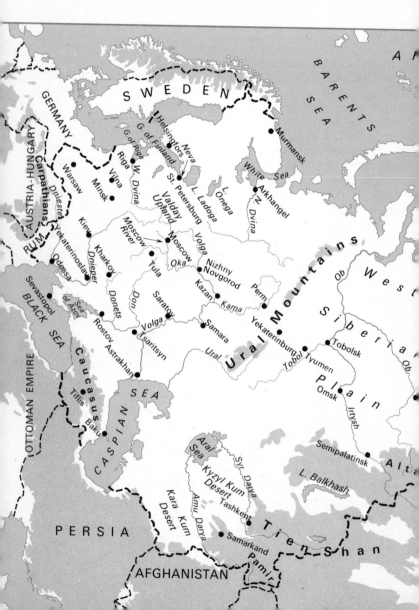

Lake Baikal, showing Peshchanaya Bay.
Baikal is the largest lake in Siberia and
the deepest in the world (5,660 ft.).
Chekhov crossed it by steamer in
1890 travelling east to Sakhalin. Here, he said, Siberia's
poetry began; hitherto all his journey had been prose.

often at the initiative of empire-building Russian military governors on the spot and in retaliation against raids by what the Russians thought of as marauding nomads. In 1868 the Emir of Bokhara was forced to yield part of his kingdom, including Samarkand, and to accept Russian protection and dependent status. He was followed by the Khan of Khiva in 1873. In 1876 the Khanate of Kokand was subdued and shortly afterwards fear of Russian designs on India led the British to look to the defences of the Khyber Pass. By 1885 Russia had also annexed the whole of Transcaspia.

By its very size imperial Russia seemed to threaten western Europe. It had some eight and a half million square miles of territory, of which about one quarter was in Europe and the remainder in Asia, so that it was larger than the entire north American continent. For a time the British Empire covered an even vaster expanse, but it was scattered over the globe. There was nowhere a continuous stretch of territory, ruled from a single centre, of comparable size to the Russian Empire. The sun did set on it – but not for many hours. Siberia above all caught the imagination of the world as a sort of European Russia writ even larger. With its vast coniferous forests, huge rivers, savage winter climate, extensive mountain ranges and general unsavoury repute, it seemed like another planet. Its area, one and a half times that of Europe including European Russia, was calculated to be greater than that of the face of the full moon.

Relief

From the point of view of physical relief, European Russia and much of Siberia together form a huge plain flanked by mountains to east and south and extending from the western frontier through sixty degrees of longitude to the River Yenisey in central Siberia. A barrier, but not an important one, is imposed by the Ural Mountains (highest point, 6,210 feet), the boundary between Russia in Europe and Russia in Asia. The Valday Upland, rising

The Imperial Russian Frontier: the Russian Empire at the beginning of the twentieth century, showing the main territorial changes which occurred during, and just before, the period under review. The main areas of expansion in the nineteenth century were: Finland (1809); Poland (1815); the Caucasus (1801–59); the Far East (1858–60); Central Asia (1853–85). The largest area ceded by Russia was Alaska, sold to the United States of America in 1867.

RUSSIA

CANADA

ALASKA

BERING SEA

PACIFIC
OCEAN

Aleutian Is.

Russian territory
sold to U.S.A. 1867

Lena

Yakutsk

SEA OF
OKHOTSK

Kamchatka

1853

Sakhalin
1875

Ceded to Japan
1905

Kurile Islands

To Japan 1875

Lena

L. Baikal

Irkutsk

Chita

Amur 1858-1860

Khabarovsk

C H I N A

Manchuria

Vladivostok

SEA
OF

JAPAN

JAPAN

0   500 Miles

0   800 Kms.

Port Arthur
(Russian 1898-1905) JAPAN

Boundary of the
Russian Empire 1914 ▬ ▬ ▬

The River Yenisey near Biryusa above Krasnoyarsk. The Yenisey is one of the three great north-flowing Siberian rivers and marks the eastern end of the great plain of central Siberia.

to little more than 1,000 feet south-east of St Petersburg, and the Central Russian Upland, to the south of Moscow, formed even less of a barrier. It is on the southern and eastern frontiers that real obstacles are found. They begin in the south-west with the Carpathian Mountains and Crimean Upland, and continue in grander style with the Caucasian chain and – beyond the Caspian – the Pamir, Tien Shan, Altay and Sayan ranges. Eastern Siberia is crossed by mountain chains, the Yablonovy, Stanovoy and others. Thus the southern border of the Empire was almost everywhere fenced off by mountains or seas.

Hydrography

Russia has the two largest lakes in the world, so large that they are termed seas: the Caspian and the Aral. Apart from these she has the largest lakes in Asia (Baikal and Balkhash) and in Europe (Ladoga and Onega).

She is well stocked with rivers too, having the longest in Europe, the Volga (2,300 miles in length), and three in Siberia that dwarf even the Volga: the Ob (3,500 miles from the source of its chief tributary, the Irtysh), the Yenisey (3,700 miles from the source of the Selenga) and the Lena (2,670 miles).

Many important rivers of European Russia rise in a small area of the western midlands formed by the Valday and Central Russian Uplands. These include the Volga and its tributary the Oka, and also the Western Dvina, Dnieper and Don. Being close to each other and easily linked by portages in early times, and later by canal, the river system provided Russia with a valuable communication network, especially as most Russian rivers are slow-flowing and navigable far upstream. But many rivers become icebound for much of the year, flood heavily in spring and form shallows in summer. And Russians often felt that their rivers did not really lead anywhere. So many pour into landlocked or partly landlocked seas: the Caspian, Sea of Azov, Black Sea, Gulf of Riga, Gulf of Finland and the White Sea. Others, including the three longest

Russia in Asia: administrative boundaries
(late nineteenth century). Since population density was so
much less than in European Russia, the administrative
areas are correspondingly larger; the Yakutsk Region
was the biggest of all and larger than
many European States.

EUROPEAN RUSSIA

Caucasus

CASPIAN SEA

Volga

Ural Mountains

TOBOLSK

S

i

YE

Tobolsk

Irtysh

Tyumen

Uralsk

Omsk

Tomsk

Krasno

TOMSK

Ob

Altay

Irtysh

URAL

TURGAY

Turgay

AKMOLINSK

Akmolinsk

Semipalatinsk

SEMIPALATINSK

L. Balkhash

Aral Sea

TRANSCASPIA

SYR-DARYA

SEMIRECHENSK

KHIVA

Khiva

SAMARKAND

Tashkent

Kokànd

Bokhara

Samarkand

Ferghana

FERGHANA

BOKHARA

Pamir

Tien Shan

Ob

rivers of Siberia, drain into the Arctic Ocean, not the most convenient of jumping-off points. Many Russian ports become icebound for long periods. So although Russians could move around effectively, if not very comfortably, inside their Empire by sledge, carriage or train, they sometimes felt claustrophobic about their restricted access to the world's sea routes.

Vegetation

Vegetationally Russia consists of uneven broad zones running in roughly horizontal bands across European Russia and Siberia. In the extreme north are the Arctic wastes and tundra, thinly populated and of slight historical importance. South of those come the two most important vegetational zones: first the forest and then, to the south of that, the steppe – the word denotes a large treeless plain or prairie covered with herbaceous vegetation and having a dry climate.

Most of the forest zone is coniferous and is sometimes called, especially with reference to Siberia, the *tayga*. But in European Russia a wedge of mixed forest, coniferous and deciduous, stretches south of the coniferous belt from the western frontier and tapers off near Kazan on the Volga. Though smaller in area, the

A view of Nizhny Novgorod on the Volga. The famous trade fair, held annually between 1817 and 1930, was the biggest in Russia and made Nizhny Novgorod the main trading centre of the Empire. The town has been renamed Gorky after its most famous son.

mixed forest is important as the cradle of the modern state, where Russia, centred on Moscow, made a second start after the decline of the old Russian state based on Kiev. Besides Moscow itself the area of mixed forest included such other historic cities as Novgorod, Nizhny Novgorod (now Gorky), Yaroslavl, Vladimir, Smolensk and St Petersburg.

As one moved southwards there was no sudden change from forest to steppe. First came a transitional area, part woods and part steppe, sometimes termed the wooded steppe or meadow-grass steppe – found, for example in Oryol Province, scene of Turgenev's *Sportsman's Sketches*. South of it comes the steppe proper, also called feather-grass steppe. This in turn blends into arid (also called saline or wormwood) steppe, merging further to the south-east with the sand or stone deserts of Central Asia.

Not being fit for cultivation, the arid steppe was thinly populated, being the preserve of pastoral nomads. But the steppe proper and the wooded steppe are good crop-raising country, coinciding partly with the fertile black earth (*chernozem*) belt which stretches from the western frontier to the Altay foothills and reaches its greatest breadth of just under two hundred miles in European Russia. This became famous as one of the world's granaries and was supporting about a hundred people to the square mile at the beginning of the twentieth century. But the incursions of raiding horsemen had hampered cultivation of these lands until fairly late in Russian history, and insufficient rainfall made the raising of crops somewhat hazardous even on black earth.

Climate

Poor conditions for growing food, the attacks of outside enemies, unsettled internal conditions and the exactions of central authority – all tended to make Russia a place where mere survival was an achievement. And there was also the Russian climate, which, as Yepikhodov rightly says in Chekhov's *Cherry Orchard* (1903–4), 'isn't exactly co-operative'.

Russia has an arctic climate in the extreme north, a subtropical climate on parts of the Black Sea coast, of Transcaucasia and of Central Asia, and a monsoon-type climate on the Pacific coast of the Far East. But these are only the fringes. The rest of the country, by far the greatest part of Russian territory, has a continental climate with long, cold winters and short, fairly hot summers. As one travels from west to east the range of temperature, between the cold of winter and the heat of summer, becomes ever wider. Eastern Siberia has an extreme continental climate. It can have heat waves in summer, but its winters are very severe, and it includes at Verkhoyansk what is often claimed as the cold pole of the northern hemisphere with a mean temperature in January of $-58°F$. and a lowest recorded temperature of $-83 \cdot 6°F$. Over most of European Russia too, winter is the longest and perhaps most typically Russian season. The average number of days with a below-zero temperature has been put at a hundred and forty and a hundred and fifty in Moscow and St Petersburg respectively, with a hundred and eighty in the middle Urals and a hundred and ninety in Archangel in the far north. Even in the southern port of Odessa the figure is as high as ninety (Schlesinger, p. 238).

Seasons

The Russian winter can be monotonous, but is also awesome and picturesque. It is rendered more bearable by a tendency for the coldest days to be windless, at least in the north and centre. In the south blizzards are more common, so that the winters there can also be severe. But for Russian society in Moscow and St Petersburg, winter was a gay time with visits to the theatre and balls, and with sleighs whirring through the streets almost silent on the snow except for the tinkling of their bells. On fine days the low sun glittered blindingly on snow and ice. To Russian merchants winter was the time when heavy loads could be transported more easily than over the atrocious ruts and mire of the roads in spring and autumn. For the peasants field work came to an end in winter, but they might take seasonal jobs in a town and their families might have work to do at home, the organisation of cottage industries being widely developed.

The beginning of winter, with the arrival of the 'new road' – for sledges instead of carts – was a glad occasion, bringing the end of autumn slush. Another exhilarating event was the onset of spring, with the bleak, silent monochrome of winter rapidly giving way to colours, smells and bird song, while the breaking ice on the rivers thundered like an artillery barrage. For the farmer the summer was all too short, the sowing and reaping of a crop often being crowded into a mere hundred days. So spurts of intense effort were needed at sowing, haymaking and harvest time, in contrast to the long periods of winter inactivity.

4 Communications

Waterways

The rivers of European Russia were linked by canals constructed in the eighteenth and nineteenth centuries, especially in the 1810s, and there was thus communication by water between the Black, Caspian, Baltic and White Seas. A cargo ship could go all the way from Astrakhan to St Petersburg with a load of seven hundred tons, covering some two thousand five hundred miles of water in forty days. But grain shipments from the south, being compelled to start in autumn, might be overtaken by winter and could reach distant destinations only in the next year. A convoy of seven or eight barges might take four thousand tons of wheat up the Volga from Samara (now Kuybyshev) to Rybinsk where it would be stored until spring and then shipped on to St Petersburg (Westwood, p. 18).

Steamships were in early use. They first appeared on the Neva in 1815 and were plying on the Volga and Dnieper by the 1820s, but it was not until the end of the century that they were used widely. Before that, traction on the Russian rivers was supplied by men and horses, with horses as the more expensive. Teams of 'Volga boatmen' hauled barges upstream by rope, or a tug attached to a train of barges would be warped upriver to an anchor taken ahead by rowing boat, the anchor rope being attached to a capstan turned by horses or teams of men.

Waterways remained the most important channel for transporting freight in bulk over a large part of the country, and were in increasing use throughout the century, despite the development of railways and some improvement in roads. By the early twentieth century Russia had over a hundred thousand miles of navigable inland waterways, carrying over thirty million tons of freight a year, as opposed to six million in 1861. Timber and firewood made up more than half the freight carried and grain about an eighth.

Rivers also carried human freight. Part of the journey to prison and penal settlement in Siberia was handled by contractors who supplied barges to convey convicts from Tyumen to Tomsk, taking them down the Irtysh and up the Ob (Kennan, p. 83). These vessels were often grossly overloaded, and their tightly packed cargo proved perishable. But for travellers less pressed river transport formed the most soothing kind of Russian journey with the occasional drama of a sandbank to relieve the gentle monotony.

Some captains, according to one nineteenth-century observer, used to carry a few 'stalwart Cossacks' free, so that they could jump overboard when the boat got stuck and pull it off 'with a stout hawser' (Mackenzie Wallace, i, p. 10). The same observer also complains of bugs on the Don steamers, of rats on the Sea of Azov and of an atmosphere of genial dirtiness everywhere. But the traveller by road was not free from dirt and vermin either, and those who could were often glad to take the boat.

Roads

Imperial Russian road haulage was mainly done by horse-power, despite the immemorial camels of the east and new-fangled electric trams, since 1880 in St Petersburg and earlier elsewhere. But travelling conditions were notoriously bad, a typical road being immensely broad, surfaced by nature only, and more a collection of ruts than a highway. Moreover carriages and carts, even those used by passengers, commonly lacked springs, so travellers would take a load of pillows, or hay might be packed in to lessen jolting. Hard-surface high-roads, called *chaussées*, were few indeed. Half way through the nineteenth century Russia had only about three thousand miles of them, and during the Crimean War the Russian army in the Crimea was more effectively cut off from its home bases than the British and French. Even by the end of the century the Empire had only some ten thousand miles of *chaussées*.

Two Russian roads were famous. The spectacular Georgian Military Road was travelled by Pushkin in 1829, as described in his *Journey to Erzerum*. It runs for about a hundred and twenty

miles through the Daryal Pass in the high Caucasus from Vladikavkaz (now Ordzhonikidze) in the north to Tiflis in the south. The other was remarkable for its length of some four thousand miles and for the misfortunes of the many exiles and convicts who trod or rode it. It led from St Petersburg through Novgorod, Moscow, Nizhny Novgorod and Kazan to Perm. Entering Siberia, it became the Siberian Highway and proceeded as far as Irkutsk. Chekhov, who travelled along it through Tyumen and Tomsk in 1890, called it the longest and ugliest road in the world.

In *Eugene Onegin* Pushkin describes a road journey made by the Larin family in central European Russia, from a country estate to Moscow, and lists some of the disadvantages. Perhaps, he says, Russia may have a network of *chaussées*, iron bridges and underwater tunnels in five hundred years time. But 'now our roads are bad. Neglected bridges rot. At post-stations you can't get a minute's sleep for bugs and fleas. There are no inns – just a pretentious, but meagre menu hanging in a cold hut for appearance's sake and mocking your futile appetite.' But, as Pushkin goes on to point out, 'travelling in the cold season of winter is pleasant and easy' (Pushkin *Eugene Onegin*, vii, verses 33–35).

Repin's famous picture of the Volga boatmen, or *burlaki*, a notoriously tough breed of men who hauled barges and boats up river. Their labour was often cheaper than horse traction.

So indeed it was – at least by comparison. With a carpet of snow and ice covering the greater part of the Empire, one could go by sledge all the way from the northern port of Archangel on the White Sea to the Caspian port of Astrakhan at the mouth of the Volga, even if many of the 'roads' consisted of no more than a row of posts to show the way. But winter travel was no joy ride either. Passengers could become seasick from swooping up and down 'waves' – transverse undulations in the snow. And open sledges were used, an ordeal in Siberian conditions, especially with a head wind – even if some thought it a thrill to be tumbled out when, as often happened, the sledge overturned into soft snow.

Many travellers have commented on the insalubrious post-stations, where one was lucky to get a place on a bench or on the floor to rest for an hour or two while other visitors drank tea, chatted, laughed, smoked and otherwise made themselves a nuisance. The post-stations were set up at intervals of ten to twenty miles along the main roads and made it possible, though not always easy, to continue one's journey on producing the *podorozhnaya*, a large warrant stamped with the imperial eagle and entitling the traveller to horses, carriage and driver to take him on

Two post-road drivers. Russian roads were of notoriously poor quality and few were metalled. Carriages and sleighs often broke down or pitched their occupants into mud or snow.

his next stage against a fixed tariff. In practice, as Russian literature testifies, travellers were often greeted at the door by the station inspector with a rude bellow: 'No horses!' But tact, bribery, patience or bullying would produce them in the end. There is a picture of these conditions in *The Station Inspector*, one of Pushkin's *Tales of Belkin* (1831), beginning: 'Who has not cursed station inspectors, who has not quarrelled with them?'

In a country so rich in waterways, bridges formed a notorious hazard to the land traveller. Mackenzie Wallace calls them a barrier, not a connecting link, and says that the cautious driver would prefer to take to the water if there was a ford near by. He has a splendid description of the sort of thing that happened when a Russian coachman crossed a bridge:

'Making hurriedly the sign of the Cross, he gathers up his reins, waves his little whip in the air, and, shouting lustily, urges on his team'. The operation is not wanting in excitement. First there is a short descent; then the horses plunge wildly through a zone of deep mud; next comes a fearful jolt as the vehicle is jerked up on to the first planks; then the transverse planks, which are but loosely held in their places, rattle and rumble ominously, as the experienced, sagacious animals pick their way cautiously and gingerly among the dangerous holes and crevices; lastly you plunge with a horrible jolt into a second mud zone, and finally regain *terra firma*, conscious of that pleasant sensation which a young officer may be supposed to feel after his first cavalry charge in real warfare (Mackenzie Wallace, i, p. 23).

Below. A convoy of prisoners marches under escort to Siberia.
Some can be seen wearing the usual ankle-fetters. The journey
from European Russia took several months and was made
mainly on foot along a series of staging-prisons. River barges,
carriages and trains (depending on the geography, the historical period
and the status of the prisoner) were also used as transport.

Privileged travellers might move faster. There are some figures
on the time taken by various Tsars to cover the four hundred and
eighty-six miles from St Petersburg to Moscow in winter conditions. Peter the Great's record stood for a long time at forty-
eight hours, but was lowered to forty-two by Alexander I in 1810.
In December 1833, according to a note in Pushkin's journal,
Nicholas I beat all records by covering the distance in thirty-eight
hours (Pushkin, *Eugene Onegin*, ed. Nabokov, iii, p. 112).

How difficult – indeed heroic – a feat journeys could be for less
august travellers is illustrated by many masterpieces of Russian
travel literature in addition to some already mentioned. They
include Chekhov's journey across Siberia to Sakhalin described in
his letters and the articles *From Siberia* (1890) written *en route*.
Anyone who wishes to know what it was like to cross Siberia in the
opposite direction at the time of the Crimean War, and get from

The Imperial Russian Railway System, showing the extent of
the permanent way in 1870, 1890 and 1914. The first major
Russian railway was the St Petersburg–Moscow line, opened
in 1851. Booms in railway building took place in the 1860s
and early 1870s; and also between 1891 and 1905, during
which time a large part of the Trans-Siberian Railway was built.

Ayan on the Sea of Okhotsk to Yakutsk, should consult the closing chapters of Goncharov's *Frigate Pallas*. To them may be added two classics of English and American nineteenth-century travel: *Ride to Khiva* by Captain Fred Burnaby of the Royal Horse Guards (1876) and George Kennan's *Siberia and the Exile System* (1891). Among numerous evocations of the Russian road in fiction are the two journeys, one fatal and one uproarious, in Tolstoy's *Master and Man* (1895) and Gogol's *Dead Souls*.

Railways

The first public railway in Russia, between St Petersburg and near-by Tsarskoye Selo (now Pushkin), the Tsar's residence, was opened in 1837. The Warsaw–Vienna line, the second to receive Nicholas I's approval, ran outside the boundaries of Russia proper, but opened opportunely in 1848 in time to carry the Russian troops used in the following year to suppress the Hungarian uprising. The first major Russian railway was the St Petersburg–Moscow line, opened in 1851. This runs in an almost straight line between the two cities, but the story that Nicholas I settled a dispute about its course by ruler and pen, even including four small kinks where his fingers stuck out over the edge of the ruler, is probably untrue (Westwood, p. 30).

At the time of the Crimean War Russia had only seven hundred and fifty miles of railway. The first Russian railway boom took place in the 1860s and early 1870s, leaving the Empire with over 14,000 miles of operating track in 1881. This was mainly the work of private firms operating under government guarantee. A further boom, associated with the building of the Trans-Siberian Railway, took place between 1891 and 1905, adding nearly 20,000 miles of new line. The second Russian railway boom was a more directly state enterprise and the treasury had also begun to buy up privately owned railway companies.

Russian trains were large. They used a wider gauge than the usual western European, and foreigners found them comfortable, but slow and late. They had double windows and doors as protection against the intense cold, and were heated by iron stoves. All carriages could be used as sleepers and there were three classes, of which the third had wooden benches. Stations were often placed inconveniently far from the towns which they were supposed to serve, as often noted in Chekhov's stories and plays. The trouble was, according to his evidence, that town councils could not always raise the large bribes which engineers and constructors required to site stations more conveniently. Apart from which, land was cheaper outside the towns.

A practice often mentioned in literature is one which outlived imperial Russia – of ringing three times on the station bell before a train left. The first (single) ring took place a quarter of an hour before departure, the second (double) ring gave five minutes' warning, and on the third (triple) peal the train pulled out.

Tolstoy's Anna Karenin committed suicide by jumping under a train, thus breaking the usual sociable and cosy conventions of the Russian railway journey. On more normal occasions there would be the conductor's samovar steaming away to provide plenty of tea. Or passengers would make their own, queuing up during halts at stations to take boiling water made available in large cauldrons.

Russian industrialisation in the late nineteenth century owed much to the railways, but they never quite caught the popular imagination as they did in north America. Russian railway building has been called a 'forced growth sponsored by the Tsar and built by foreigners' (Westwood, p. 7), which is perhaps to overstate the case, but it is true that the state provided much of the initiative and finance, including the proceeds of selling Alaska to the United States in 1867.

5 Peoples

A multinational state

Western Europeans of the nineteenth century often thought that there were too many Russians in the world. Writing in the 1880s, when Russia's population stood at about 115 millions, Leroy-Beaulieu pointed out that Russia then had twice as many citizens as the most populous among the other Christian countries (Leroy-Beaulieu, i, p. 5). A Russian authority on military affairs writing in 1900 called the Empire's reserves of manpower 'downright inexhaustible', and added a warning that she could easily maintain a standing army of two and a half million if she wished to make 'as great an effort as certain western European states' (Kovalevsky, p. 953). Population, by territorial expansion and natural increase, was growing fast from about thirty-six millions in 1796 to the nearly one hundred and twenty-six million, excluding Finland with over two and a half million, recorded in the census of 1897. This was an increase of three and a half times in a century. Leroy-Beaulieu had earlier worked out that the population would reach one hundred and eighty million by about 1950, but seems to have underestimated (Leroy-Beaulieu, i, p. 41).

By no means all these people were Russians, though foreigners often assumed that they were, just as the same natural mistake is still made about citizens of the Soviet Union, and just as the uninitiated insist on regarding Scotsmen, Welshmen and Irishmen as English. In fact the person whom the uninitiated foreigner called a Russian might really be a Lithuanian peasant, a Georgian prince, a nomad Kalmyk, a Tungus from eastern Siberia, or in an extreme case a Polish count. Some of these, certainly the Polish count, would be quick to correct such error. Others might not bother, while some from remoter parts might scarcely have clapped eyes on Russians and know them only by repute.

The Empire contained a mixture of races professing many religions and speaking a profusion of tongues. No attempt will be made even to list all the peoples and languages involved, but a review of the most important is essential. Such a survey must be

The distribution of peoples in Imperial Russia, as seen by a late nineteenth-century cartographer (from Brockhaus and Efron's Entsiklopedichesky slovar; vol. xxvii: St Petersburg, 1899). The greater part of the population consisted of Slavs, with Russians (about 45 % of the whole population) predominant, followed by Ukrainians, Poles and Belorussians. About a third of the population consisted of non-Slavs, of

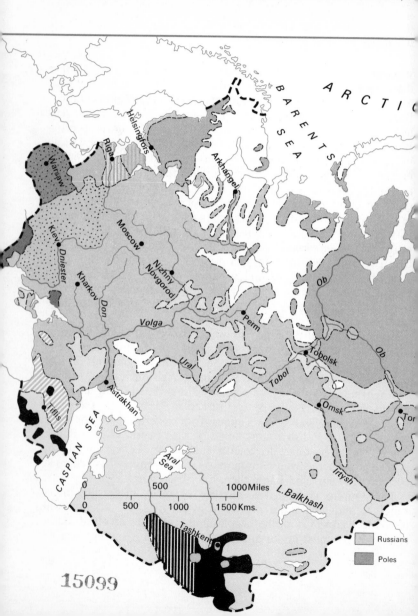

15099

which the Turkic peoples were the most numerous. Finnic peoples, Jews, Germans, Armenians, Georgians, Latvians, Lithuanians, and Rumanians within the Empire all numbered over a million at the end of the nineteenth century.

Lithuanians and Latvians

Teutonic peoples (Germans, Swedes) and Rumanians

Turkic peoples and Mongols (also Chinese and Koreans)

Iranians (Tadzhiks in Turkestan; Ossetians;Tats; Kurds; Armenians in the Caucasus)

Jews

Tunguses, Manchurians and related peoples

Caucasians (Georgians etc., West and East Caucasian mountain tribes)

Finnic peoples(Western Finns, Vorga Finns, Kama Finns, Finno-Ugrians and Samoyeds)

Peoples of unknown or American origin (Yenisey Ostyaks, Ainos, Gilyaks, Kamchadals, Yukagirs, Koryaks, Chukchi)

Below left. A Kirgiz potentate. Most of the Kirgiz, who were Mohammedans, were nomads. They wandered the steppes of east European and central Asiatic Russia and correspond in part to what are now known as Kazakhs, as well as to the modern Kirgiz. *Below right*. A Kalmyk (or Calmuck) girl. The Kalmyks, a Mongolian-speaking people of Buddhist religion, were nomads in the area of the lower Volga. Their religious leader was a Grand Lama.

russo-centric, which means that many minority peoples of the Empire will be briefly dismissed. The Slavs, who formed the core of the population, will be considered first, and after them the non-Slav peoples.

The East Slavs

Apart from the Poles (considered below, p. 76), the Slav peoples of the Empire belonged to the East Slav branch. They are now three distinct peoples: Russians, Ukrainians and Belorussians. But in the nineteenth century this distinction was less clear and many Ukrainians and Belorussians simply thought of themselves as Russians. Certainly all three peoples were lumped together as Russian by imperial officials, foreign historians and guide-books such as Baedeker's.

Under the Tsars the Ukrainians were officially known as Little Russians and the Ukraine was called Little Russia. The term

Below left. A Tatar from Tomsk in Siberia. The majority of the Tatars lived in the Caucasus (the modern Azerbaydzhanis), on the Volga and in the Crimea. *Below right*. Interior of Terek Cossack hut. The Cossacks were of mixed origin, being chiefly descended from Russian or Ukrainian peasants who had fled to the periphery of the Empire away from serfdom and other exactions of the central state.

Ukraine does go back at least to the seventeenth century, but it was not until the nineteenth century and under the influence of the Ukrainian national movement, that Ukrainians began to call themselves such. Besides those who simply thought of themselves as Russian, many also called themselves Cossacks, and they used the term Muscovites (*moskali*) to describe Russians in the more restricted sense, otherwise known as Great Russians. In return Muscovites called them top-knots (*khokhly*).

The term Great Russian is literary, not colloquial, and was used in the nineteenth century to describe what are now just called Russians, when it was necessary to differentiate them from Ukrainians and Belorussians. It is still sometimes convenient to use the term Great Russian to avoid confusion. Strictly speaking it is literature written in the Great Russian language – not the literature of the Ukraine or Belorussia – to which the present study presents a background. The Belorussians are, incidentally, sometimes referred to as White Russians, which is natural since Russian

bely means 'white', but can lead to confusion owing to the use of the same term to describe the opponents of the Reds in the Russian Civil War of 1917–22, and also decreasingly to describe emigrants from the USSR in general.

One further point must be stressed. Nationality was more closely connected with religion than it is in the officially anti-religious Soviet Union. Any subject of the Tsar, professing the Orthodox faith, tended to be considered a Russian, whatever his racial origin, if he spoke Russian as his first language. Religion, language, domicile and citizenship made you a Russian. Race or the shape of your eyes, nose and cheekbones were unimportant.

In the old Russian State based on Kiev between the ninth and thirteenth centuries, there were tribal distinctions, but none closely corresponding to the present distinctions between Great Russian, Ukrainian and Belorussian. These are the result of separate historical evolution since Kievan times and owe much to the fact that the ancestors of the Ukrainians and Belorussians came under the Tatars briefly or not at all, but were under Lithuanian and Polish rule for several centuries.

The relative numbers of the three peoples are indicated by figures based on the census taken in 1897, at which time the total population of the Empire stood at about 128 million:

Nineteenth century name	Population	Modern name
Great Russian	c. 55·7 million	Russian
Little Russian	c. 22·4 million	Ukrainian
Belorussian	c. 5·9 million	Belorussian
TOTAL: Russians	c. 84·0 million	

Thus Great Russians, Ukrainians and Belorussians together formed about two thirds of the Empire's population at the end of the nineteenth century. Great Russians on their own came to about 45 per cent of the total and were thus themselves a minority people.

Muscovy and imperial Russia

Moscow began its career as an appanage princedom dependent on the near-by great princedom of Vladimir. But the princes of Moscow gradually took over neighbouring territory, aided by their central geographical position and convenient access to the main river routes. This process was well advanced by 1480, in which year Moscow ceased to pay tribute to the Tatars and thus formally became the centre of an independent Muscovite state. Muscovy continued to expand. Before the accession of Ivan the Terrible in 1533 it had taken over all other previously autonomous Russian territories except those ruled by Lithuania and Poland. Ivan took the title Tsar of All Russia in 1547 and greatly extended Muscovite control by conquering Tatar lands in Kazan, Astrakhan and Siberia. Further expansion into Siberia and the incorporation of part of the Ukraine into the Muscovite state followed in the seventeenth century.

It is from Peter the Great (ruled 1689–1725) that the beginning of the imperial period of Russian history dates. He transformed and modernised the country, replacing Moscow as capital with the newly-founded St Petersburg in 1712, which, renamed Petrograd in 1914, remained the capital until 1918 when Moscow resumed its old status. In a sense Moscow had never quite lost it owing to the practice of calling the two greatest cities the two capitals.

Ukrainians

Ukrainians had an especially turbulent history, being ruled by, quarrelled over and partitioned among Turks, Poles, Austrians and Great Russians, rebelling and intriguing against all, and falling gradually within the expanding Russian state. If Ukrainians must be ruled by others, it was the Great Russians, also members of the Orthodox Church, that they preferred. In 1654 the Ukrainian Cossack Bogdan Khmelnitsky, leader of a successful revolt against Poland, brought large parts of the Ukraine into union with

Muscovy in addition to those already under Muscovite control. There was argument later about the degree of autonomy accorded to Ukrainians by this arrangement. In any case they were incorporated in the imperial state in the reign of Catherine the Great, when the three partitions of Poland brought Belorussia and the remaining Polish-ruled parts of the Ukraine within the Russian Empire, except Galicia, which went to Austria.

Catherine's reign also saw Russian rule established over large territories on the Black Sea coast, including the Crimea, which had been under Turkish control. Called New Russia, a name now obsolete, these provinces were colonised by Ukrainians, Russians and others including Greeks, Bulgarians and Germans. The Ukrainians, who suffered from overpopulation, helped to colonise the North Caucasus and Siberia. Serfdom was introduced into the Ukraine, and Ukrainian officers became serf-owning aristocrats admitted to the status of gentry in Russian law.

Ukrainian nationalism, aspiring to autonomy within the Empire or to full independence, arose in the 1840s under the influence of the Ukrainian poet Taras Shevchenko. The Polish revolt of 1863 led the Russian government to restrict local cultures, and from

Kuban Cossacks in 1837 at Taman, at the western end of the military line held by the Cossacks for defence and attack against the tribes of the Caucasus, some of which were still 'savage', i.e. independent of Russia.

1876 to 1905 it was illegal to publish anything in Ukrainian except folk-lore material. Whether Ukrainian is an independent language or a mere dialect of Russian is a question which exercised both Ukrainians and Russians, often being judged more by political than linguistic criteria. Among the great Russian writers Gogol was of Ukrainian origin, and his two early collections of stories, *Evenings on a Farm near Dikanka* (1831–2) and *Mirgorod* (1835), are set in the Ukraine and draw on Ukrainian folk-lore and history, but are written in Russian.

Cossacks

As reference to Gogol reminds one, Cossacks often figure in Russian literature, but without non-Russian readers always being clear who they were. They were not a separate people, but Russians or Ukrainians who absorbed other ethnic elements as well, being mainly descendants of peasants of Orthodox faith, who had fled to the frontiers to escape serfdom, taxes and (in the case of those evading Polish rule), religious and national persecution.

Cossack (*kazak*) comes from a Turkic word meaning 'free man, warrior', and their original communities had arisen by the sixteenth century on the Rivers Dnieper, Don and Ural (then called Yaik) as self-governing bodies engaged in hunting, fishing, pillaging and conducting guerrilla warfare against Turk and Tatar. In the seventeenth century they turned to agriculture. The same century also saw the revolt of Stenka Razin (1670), followed just over a hundred years later by that of Pugachov (1773), the participants in both uprisings being largely Cossacks. Pushkin wrote a *History of the Pugachov Rebellion* (1834) and brought Pugachov and his revolt into the novel *The Captain's Daughter* (1836). The most famous Cossack community was the 'Sech' of the Zaporozhian Cossacks on the lower Dnieper, which is described by Gogol in *Taras Bulba* (1835), set in the seventeenth century. The Sech was abolished by Catherine the Great in 1775, and its chief *ataman* (leader) Kalnishevsky immured in the Solovetsky Monastery.

As this shows, the state clamped down hard on the Cossacks in the eighteenth century, when they also began to be used as more regular frontier forces. Cossack communities were founded by the central government in the north Caucasus, in the areas of Astrakhan and Orenburg, and in parts of Siberia. Cossack leaders, once elected in popular assembly, and senior officers, came to be appointed by the Tsar or war ministry and the Cossacks acquired their own landowning aristocracy. The Don Cossacks were their chief community, supplying in the early twentieth century seventeen of the thirty-five Cossack regiments in the peacetime Russian army. The Cossacks became pillars of the state, regarded as the Tsar's most loyal soldiers and used as riot police to suppress political and labour disorders. They performed compulsory military service, each providing his own horse and equipment in return for privileges which included tax exemption.

Because of their romantic past as turbulent pioneers, with the marches of the Empire as a sort of Russian 'wild east', these were picturesque figures to compatriots in the hinterland, who could read a vivid contemporary account of them in Tolstoy's *Cossacks* in addition to the historical fiction and other works of Pushkin and Gogol mentioned above.

Siberia

Siberia usually denoted the Russian Empire east of the Urals, excluding Central Asia. Though containing many indigenous peoples, it became predominantly Slav after colonisation had begun in the sixteenth century when Russians probed these vast territories to get salt, fish and furs. In 1581 the mercantile family of the Stroganovs mounted an expedition led by the Cossack Yermak, who achieved the conquest of Siberia by defeating a local ruler, the Siberian Khan Kuchum. In 1639 another Cossack, Ivan Moskvityanin, reached the Pacific Ocean.

The Siberian tribes could not resist Russian expansion, but many still survived, including the Buryats (Buddhists or Christians who speak a language akin to Mongol); the Yakuts (who speak a Turkic language), and the partly nomad, hunting, fishing, reindeer-breeding Tunguses and Chuckchis.

Since the eighteenth century Siberia has been a place of exile and imprisonment for criminal and political offenders, including many writers. Siberians enjoyed more freedom than European Russians – partly because none of them could be 'sent to Siberia' (since they were already there), and the institution of serfdom did not operate there.

Siberia had a much sparser population than European Russia, but was growing faster, from just over a million in 1800 to the five and three quarter millions recorded in the 1897 census. Towards the end of the century these vast territories were being more and more colonised, especially in the west, by settlers from overpopulated parts of southern Great Russia and the Ukraine. The movement enjoyed a varying amount of official support, and after the famine of 1891 and the building of the Trans-Siberian Railway, mainly in 1891–9, the number of immigrants swelled to over a hundred thousand a year. In parts of Siberia peasants could find steppe, including black earth, in conditions resembling those of their old homes. Would-be immigrants were at one time obliged to send scouts ahead to pick land which could be reserved till the main body came along.

A well-known description of Siberia is that in Dostoyevsky's *Notes from the House of the Dead*, describing his own life, thinly disguised as fiction, for four years as a convict in the prison at Omsk. Vladimir Korolenko also drew on Siberian experiences, as an exile to the remote Yakut Region, in his story *Makar's Dream* (1885). Missionary activity in eastern Siberia forms the theme of Leskov's story *On the Edge of the World* (1889), based on the real-life experiences of Nil, Archbishop of Irkutsk, and the hero of Tolstoy's *Resurrection* follows the heroine to Siberia. To the nineteenth-century literature of Siberia must be added Chekhov's sociological study *Sakhalin Island* (1893) and other writings referred to above (p. 61).

Poles

Areas which, according to one's point of view, were Russian, Polish, Belorussian, Jewish or Ukrainian were brought into the Russian Empire by the partitions of Poland at the end of the eighteenth century, and the greater part of the Duchy of Warsaw, including Warsaw itself, followed after the Congress of Vienna (1814–5). Known in Russian as the Polish Tsardom, this came under harsher Russian control after the Polish insurrections which broke out in 1830 and 1863 and could only be quelled by major military campaigns resulting in the exile of many Poles to Siberia. The Poles were proud of their nationality, civilisation and Catholic religion, and felt that Poland was entitled to large tracts of territory which Russians looked on as theirs. Thus the two comic Poles in Dostoyevsky's *Brothers Karamazov* refuse to drink a toast to Russia without the reservation 'in its boundaries before 1772'. As an extreme Russian nationalist, Dostoyevsky often brought in such 'absurd little Poles' as minor characters. In a more truculent spirit, Pushkin had taken the opportunity of the Polish revolt of 1830–1 to tell western Europeans not to meddle in inter-Slav quarrels in his great denunciatory lyric *To Russia's Calumniators* (1831). Poland brought out the chauvinist in many Russians, but the Poles found some support among liberal-minded Russians, of whom Herzen was one. And a late story by Tolstoy, *What for?* (1906), gives a sympathetic presentation of Poles involved in the insurrection of 1830–1, providing a pleasant contrast with Pushkin's harshness. At the end of the century the number of Poles in the Empire was about nine million.

Non-Slavs (general)

About a third of the Empire's population consisted of non-Slavs, among whom Turkic peoples, recorded as over fourteen million in the 1897 census, were most numerous – about eleven per cent of the total. Finnic peoples came next with some five and a half million, almost equalled by the Jews. Other non-Slav peoples, numbering over a million at the end of the century, were Germans, Armenians, Georgians, Latvians, Lithuanians and Rumanians.

Turkic-speaking and Mohammedan peoples

Turkey itself was an independent state often in conflict with Russia, but the Russian Empire contained large groups speaking Turkic languages and belonging to the category Turkic of which the Turks of Turkey form only one subdivision. Among these were the Tatars, closely linked with the Russians from early times. Some English proverbs impute ferocity to the Tatar, but those of nineteenth-century Russia were known for their sobriety and domestic virtues, being more commonly engaged in peaceful agriculture than in slitting throats. They were used in positions of trust, as watchmen, caretakers and domestic servants, and fashionable St Petersburg restaurants used to recruit waiters from the Tatars of Ryazan Province.

Earlier Tatars had been more apt with bow and arrow than with napkin and corkscrew, being indeed of wilder origin than their sober nineteenth-century occupations suggest. They were descendants of the raiding horsemen who formed the invading armies of the Golden Horde, the Mongol-Tatar state set up in the thirteenth century by Batu Khan, a grandson of Genghiz Khan. Reaching the Volga in 1236 after huge conquests to east and south, they overran most of old Russia during the next four years and kept it under tribute, but not occupation, for nearly two and a half centuries. To this period the terms Mongol invasion and Tatar yoke are both applied, indicating that two distinct peoples were involved. In fact the Mongols were a small ruling class, and it was Turkic-speaking peoples, later called Tatars, who supplied the bulk of the armies and assimilated the ruling Mongol minority.

The Tatars were converted to Islam and formed separate states (Khanates) of which the two most important were those of the Crimea and Kazan – the latter conquered by Russia in the six-

teenth century, as were also the Tatar Khanates of Astrakhan and Siberia. Tatars and Russians lived side by side on the Volga and elsewhere, some assimilation taking place, and though difference of religion hindered the process, certain ruling Tatar families founded aristocratic lines as Russian princes. The Crimean Khanate, at first independent, became part of the Ottoman Empire in the fifteenth century, and it was not until 1783 that Russia annexed the Crimea. One popular Russian work set in Tatar Crimea was Pushkin's poem, *The Fountain of Bakhchisaray* (1824).

In the nineteenth century the term Tatar was applied to the Kazan (or Volga) Tatars, numbering 1·7 million in the 1897 census, who may be considered the descendants of Batu's Golden Horde. It was also given to the Transcaucasian Tatars (as they were then called), numbering some two million – the ancestors of the modern Azerbaydzhanis; and also to the Crimean Tatars, numbering about two hundred thousand, and to the small group of Siberian Tatars living in western Siberia.

Left. A Tatar family at home. Turkic-speaking peoples, of whom the Tatars were the most important, formed the largest non-Slav element in the Empire. The Tatars were once the conquerors of Russia, but eventually came to be valued as waiters and domestic servants.
Below. The main street of Bakhchisaray in Tatar Crimea, in 1837.

Confusion can be created when the word Tatar is loosely applied to all Mohammedan inhabitants of the Russian Empire, most of whom were also Turkic-speaking. There were some twelve million Mohammedans in all at the beginning of the twentieth century. Many had been brought in recently through Russian conquests in central Asia during the second half of the nineteenth century – Turkmens, Uzbeks, Kara-Kalpaks and many others.

It is impossible to trace all these peoples in a brief study, especially as comment is bedevilled by more recent developments and by complex changes of name and frontier. One of the most numerous Mohammedan, Turkic-speaking (but not Tatar) peoples of the nineteenth century were the Kirgiz-Kaysaks, as they were then called. These, however, correspond to the modern Kazakhs (itself, to make matters worse, a variant of the word

80

A Mordva girl. The Mordva, who lived along the middle Volga, were among the most important of the many Finnic peoples scattered over the Empire. Many of the Empire's Finns were converted to Orthodox Christianity, gradually lost their identity and became assimilated with the Great Russians.

Cossack) and not, as might be thought, to the modern Kirgiz, the main inhabitants of the present-day Union Republic of Kirgizia, who were known in the nineteenth century as the Kara-Kirgiz. The Kara-Kirgiz too were Mohammedan and Turkic-speaking, but less numerous – probably less than two hundred thousand to some four million of the Kirgiz-Kaysaks, who wandered the steppes of east European and Central Asiatic Russia. A period as a prisoner of the nomad Kirgiz forms one of the hero's adventures in Leskov's *Enchanted Wanderer* (1873).

The Bashkirs, another Turkic-speaking and Mohammedan people, were of mixed Finno–Ugrian and Turkic origin with a Mongolian admixture too. They numbered over half a million in the early twentieth century, being agriculturalists and nomads who lived in the south Urals in the area of the present Autonomous Republic of Bashkiria. The Bashkir steppe and Ufa, the main town, are the scene of S. T. Aksakov's family reminiscences disguised as fiction, *Family Chronicle* and *The Childhood of Bagrov the Grandson*. The Chuvash of the middle Volga, the area which is now the Chuvash Autonomous Republic, were another Turkic-speaking people, but were unusual in practising Orthodox Christianity by contrast with the Mohammedan affiliations of most Turkic-speakers.

Circassian women. The Circassians lived in the west Caucasus. Circassian girls were famous for their beauty and much prized in Turkish harems.

Mongolian peoples

Russia also had two Mongolian-speaking peoples of Buddhist religion, one in Europe and one in Asia. Of these the Buryats of south-eastern Siberia have been mentioned above. The others were the Kalmyks, nomads of the lower Volga, who numbered about one hundred and thirty thousand in the early twentieth century, when they roamed the arid steppes with their tents, camels and flocks. They looked somewhat like Chinese and were easily distinguished from Tatars. Their religious leader was a Grand Lama, who came to be appointed by the Russian Tsar from the beginning of the twentieth century. They enjoyed local autonomy under the governor of Astrakhan.

Finnic peoples

Finland itself was part of the Russian Empire between 1808–9, when it was annexed from Sweden, and 1917, when it obtained independence. But as a separate Grand Duchy under a governor-general appointed by the Tsar, it enjoyed internal autonomy with its own laws and a sense of national identity. The impact of the small Russian population, only about six thousand at the beginning of

the twentieth century, was slight. The Finns of Finland numbere
over two and a half million at the end of the nineteenth centur
Finnish scenery and the misfortunes of a Finnish girl seduced by
Russian officer, form themes in the poem *Eda* (1824–5) by Ye. A
Baratynsky. But though under Russian control, Finland was
foreign country, and it does not figure much in the main works c
Russian nineteenth-century literature, which tended to be russo
centric.

Apart from the Finns of Finland, whose frontier reached t
St Petersburg, there were many Finnish villages on Russian soil i
the region of the capital, which was sometimes spoken of as
Russian island in a Finnish sea. But it must be remembered tha
the Russians of St Petersburg greatly outnumbered the Finn
around them. Not far away to the west the Estonians, numberin
nearly a million in the late nineteenth century, represented anothe
branch of the Baltic Finns.

It was not the Baltic Finns who most affected Russian evolution
but their kinsmen resident on Russian territory and belonging t
the wider grouping termed Finnic. The Baltic Finns themselves ar
only one subdivision of these, admittedly the most advanced an
nationally self-conscious. To the Finnic groups also belonged man
pockets of peoples on different cultural levels, scattered about th
country. They showed varying degrees of assimilation with th
dominant Slavs, with each other, and with Turkic and othe
peoples.

Finnic tribes were the earlier occupants of the forests centred or
Moscow which became the cradle of the Great Russian state. Tc
what extent was this sparse population annihilated, driven out o
absorbed by the advancing Slav? No one can say exactly, but the
general agreement is that it was to a great extent absorbed. It has
been asserted that the Great Russians, as opposed to the Ukrain
ians and Belorussians, tend to have Finnic physical features, ir
particular flat faces with high cheek bones. The Finnic tribes, too
left behind many place names in areas which seemed to be purel
Great Russian. The very name Moscow (*Moskva*), though o

disputed etymology, has been ascribed to a Finnic origin. And as several nineteenth-century observers have illustrated, it was possible to find Finnic villages in every stage of linguistic and cultural assimilation to the Russians. Yet there are, curiously, few Finnic loan-words in Russian. So far as cultural influence is concerned, the Finns found it more blessed to receive than to give.

There were Finnic settlements along the Volga from Nizhny Novgorod to Samara – those of the Mordva, scattered over a larger area than that of the present-day Mordva Autonomous Republic, and of the Cheremis, now called Mari, situated in the area of the present-day Mari Autonomous Republic. Further east, near Perm, were the Finnic Votyaks (now called Udmurts) and the Zyryans and Permyaks (now called Komi and Komi-Permyaks respectively). Two small peoples, the Ostyaks (now called Khanty) and Voguls (now called Mansi) further complicate the picture by being of Ugrian origin, that is, belonging to the larger and more nebulous category of Finno–Ugrians, to which the Magyars of Hungary belong. Most of these peoples had been converted to the Orthodox faith, which assisted their assimilation by the Russians. The Finnic peoples abandoned their original primitive religion for Orthodox Christianity and were thus more easily absorbed by Russians than the Turkic peoples, who tended to hold on to their Mohammedan faith.

The conversion of Finnic peoples to Orthodoxy was not always as smooth as Russians liked to think. Herzen describes how the Russian police and clergy combined to blackmail the Votyaks in the area of Perm. Every few years a police officer and a priest would tour the villages to check how many Votyaks had been going to church, for they still hankered after their old, pagan religion, though supposedly converted to Orthodoxy. Herzen says that they were flogged, fined and put in prison, while the 'spiritual detective and earthly missionary . . . raise a huge ransom . . . then go away, leaving everything as it was, so as to have a chance to come back again a year or two later, with their birch and cross' (*My Past and Thoughts*, ch. XV).

Below. Jewish merchants in Odessa in the 1830s. The Jews were subject to increasing restrictions as the nineteenth century wore on. They were confined to a pale of settlement, subjected to a quota for admission to institutes of higher learning and attacked in local pogroms which the central authorities did not try very hard to stop. Massive Jewish emigration followed.

Jews

As mentioned above, the partitions of Poland at the end of the eighteenth century brought Russia large new territories in the west. With them came a Jewish population estimated at about a million. So far there had been few Jews in Russia, where permanent residence had been denied to them by law, including an edict of 1762.

The Jewish population increased faster than that of the Empire as a whole, and it has been claimed that a half of the total number of Jews in the late nineteenth century were subjects of the Tsar. The Russian government did not find a satisfactory policy for dealing with them, and they became a major social problem, or were made into one by the authorities. Jewish religion, dress, culture, education and language (a dialect of German, the forerunner of modern Yiddish) all seemed to set them apart. They

usually had recognisably Jewish names too, and as a result of all this Jews stood out as a separate people. Any tendency towards assimilation was checked by the increasingly severe disabilities imposed on them by the government.

The chief restriction was confinement to a ghetto territory, the so-called pale of settlement, consisting of certain provinces of the western and southern Empire in addition to the Jews' old homes in Poland. Even inside the pale, Jews were required to reside in towns or urban settlements, and not in villages, while in the towns themselves they might be limited to specific quarters, as was the case in Kiev, Sevastopol and Nikolayev. From the resort of Yalta they were entirely banned. There were exceptions to these residence limitations at certain times, so that Jewish communities grew up in Moscow and St Petersburg. Among those permitted to reside outside the pale were merchants of the First Guild (see p. 176) and their retainers, as well as dispensers, apothecaries and some classes of craftsmen, as also Jews with university degrees. These last were not easily come by, since another disability, imposed in 1887, was a quota for the admission of Jews to institutes of higher learning – ten per cent within the pale, five per cent outside – except that in Moscow and St Petersburg the quota was only three per cent.

Jews were resented for their alien religion and culture, or as commercial rivals, money-lenders, tax-collecting agents, vendors of hard liquor and generally as exploiters. But they were themselves exploited by Russian officials, whom they often had to bribe, and by the system of treating them as second-class citizens. They were even officially classed, together with certain primitive Asiatic tribes, as aliens (*inorodtsy*; literally 'those of other race'). In addition to their disadvantages in law, many lived in shocking poverty in appalling slums. And in the late nineteenth century anti-Jewish riots took place, especially in south and west Russia, including Odessa, and also Kishinyov, where there was a particularly bad pogrom in 1903. These pogroms were directed mainly against property, though fatal casualties were by no means unknown – some fifty people were killed and several hundred injured in the Kishinyov pogrom. Whether or not the authorities actively encouraged pogroms – and on a local level this clearly did occur – the government could probably have stopped them quite easily if it had wished.

Jews could escape some of their disabilities by being converted to Orthodox Christianity, which entitled them to 'normal' civil rights, for what that was worth in imperial Russia. But a Jew was always liable to molestation, and a particularly cruel measure was the sudden expulsion from Moscow of about twenty thousand Jews, some two thirds of the city's Jewish community, in 1891 (Greenberg, ii, p. 44). On a more anecdotal level a British Jew who was also a member of parliament, Sir Samuel Montagu, was once ordered to leave Moscow within twenty-four hours (Clarkson, p. 387), and there was the well-known story of the Jewish girl from the pale who could only pursue her studies, which involved residence in St Petersburg, by taking out a 'yellow ticket' – registering herself as a prostitute. It is not surprising that Jews emigrated in large numbers, or that Jewish intellectuals became prominent in the growing Russian revolutionary movement in the 1890s.

In nineteenth-century Russian literature Jews figure less than their numbers and importance seem to warrant. One reason for this is territorial. Most major literary works are set in Russia outside the pale of settlement and therefore in areas where most Jews could not legally reside. Where Jews do appear, reference to the scene of the action often shows that it is set at some place or time where residence restrictions on Jews did not operate. Thus an early story by Turgenev, *The Jew* (1847), is set in Danzig in 1813 and consists of the war reminiscences of a Russian colonel. Or the scene may be in the Ukraine, as in the seventeenth-century pogrom described with apparent relish by Gogol in *Taras Bulba* – the one from which his comic Jewish character Yankel manages to extricate himself. As this work vividly reminds the reader, the Cossacks were traditionally anti-Semitic.

One leading Russian writer too was strongly anti-Semitic –

Dostoyevsky, whose *Diary of a Writer* contains many violent denunciations of the Jews. This attitude is confirmed by his correspondence, but is little reflected in his novels. Jews occasionally figure in Chekhov's stories, for instance the innkeeper Moses in *Steppe* (1888) and one of the protagonists in *Rothschild's Fiddle* (1894). The plot of his play *Ivanov* (1887–9) hinges on the marriage of a Russian landowner to a Jewish girl, Sarah, who gave up her religion and family and changed her first name to the 'Christian' name Anna.

Besides the Jews of western Russia, imperial expansion also incorporated other much smaller Jewish communities: the Krymchaks of the Crimea, the Georgian Jews, the mountain Jews of the Caucasus and those of Bokhara in Central Asia. These differed from western Jews in speaking the local languages of their areas, and were descended from immigrants of medieval or ancient times.

Germans

Germans formed an important minority within the Empire, numbering about two million in the early twentieth century, to which must be added some three hundred thousand German or Austrian subjects resident in Russia. Among German subjects of Russia, the Baltic Germans of the provinces of Estland, Livland and Kurland, numbering some three hundred thousand, were an influential group. The majority of the local population consisted of Estonians and Latvians, but Germans were culturally and economically dominant, and were large landowners. Baltic Germans rose to high rank in the Russian civil service, where they had the reputation of being diehard conservatives and bureaucrats. This was not always deserved, for not all of them were Benckendorffs. In any case the anti-German policy adopted by the Russian government in the 1880s caused their influence to decrease. They usually remained Lutheran by religion and did not readily assimilate with Russians.

Aloofness was also practised by the German settlers, nearly one million in the early twentieth century, who farmed the lower Volga (the 'Volga Germans'), south European Russia – especially near Odessa – Bessarabia and parts of the Caucasus. Lutheran or Mennonite by religion, these colonists, as they were called, had been officially encouraged to settle in Russia in the late eighteenth and early nineteenth centuries. Their houses, churches and clothes were usually German in style, their settlements and villages had names like Mannheim and Zürich and they spoke their native tongue, usually a south German dialect. A typical German farming settlement was thought of as a prosperous island within a sea of feckless Slavs, whose agricultural methods and implements were often inferior.

Germans were employed in managerial positions. They were also influential as scholars and scientists, both by working and teaching in Russia themselves and through the common practice whereby young Russians, of whom Turgenev was one, studied at German universities. The Germans were better known in Russia than any other foreigners, being both admired and resented. Men of action in Russian literature tended to seem implausible unless they were given non-Russian names – preferably German, like Stolz in Goncharov's *Oblomov*. But Russians also liked to make fun of the efficient, calculating German, and a classic picture of a comic clash between Teuton and Slav is found in Leskov's story *An Iron Will* (1876) with its memorable picture of a discomfited German, Hugo Karlovich Pektoralis.

Another grotesque story of Slav and Teuton, and one which was taken from real life, is that told by Herzen about the visit of a certain Count Essen to Vladimir to preside over conscription into the army. A peasant elder, who wanted a favour done, foolishly offered this German general a bribe. But 'unluckily our Count . . . was brought up in the school of the Baltic aristocracy, which taught German loyalty to the Russian sovereign.' Count Essen lost his temper, shouted and sent for the gendarmes, and the wretched peasant, who could not conceive of anyone in uniform refusing a bribe, was so nonplussed that he let himself be hauled off to the police station without so much as a word of protest. The general himself had only wanted to teach the man a lesson, not to have him flogged and sent to Siberia, as seemed certain to happen. But the wheels of Russian bureaucracy were hard to stop, once set in motion. It was Herzen, with his better knowledge of how things were done, who sorted this business out and saved the unfortunate peasant. Absurdly enough, he himself was confined to Vladimir as an exile at the time when he performed this kindness (*My Life and Thoughts*, ch. XV).

The Caucasus

To many Russian writers the Caucasus was the most fascinating corner of the Empire, and a greater contrast with the Russian plain was not easy to imagine. In the narrow sense the name Caucasus applies to the mountain chain of the Great Caucasus, about seven hundred and fifty miles long, running from the Black Sea in the north-west to the Caspian in the south-east and reaching the height of 18,470 feet with Mount Elbrus. More generally the Caucasus denotes a larger area, including some territory (Cis-caucasia) north of the central range and more extensive lands to the south (Transcaucasia), among which are Georgia, Armenia and Azerbaydzhan.

There is probably no area on the face of the globe with a greater diversity of ethnic origins and languages than the Caucasus. This applies especially to the mountain peoples, who include amongst many others the Lezgians of Dagestan; the Chechens in the east; and the Abkhazians and Circassians in the west. Of the two ancient Christian peoples of Caucasia, the Georgians were closest to Russians by religion, since they practised the Orthodox faith, having been converted to Christianity in the year 318. The Armenians, converted even earlier to Christianity, had their own Armenian Gregorian Church. Many other peoples of the Caucasus, including the Tatars (Azerbaydzhanis) mentioned above among

Turkic-speaking peoples, and a lot of the mountain tribes, were Mohammedan.

During the first six decades of the century it was possible to fight in the Caucasus, like young Tolstoy, against 'savage' (still independent) mountain tribes on Russia's equivalent of the British North-West Frontier in India. Here at Pyatigorsk Russia's greatest romantic poet Lermontov met his death in a duel. Lermontov's novel *A Hero of Our Time* and his poems *The Demon* (completed 1839) and *Mtsyri* (1840) are among the romantic literary works inspired by this wild and picturesque territory. Pushkin's *Prisoner of the Caucasus* (1822) was also inspired by the romantic south, as was Tolstoy's posthumous novel *Hadji Murat* and some of his earliest stories. In general the Caucasus fulfilled a role like that of the English Lakes for the English Lakeland poets, though the atmosphere was more high-spirited. It was not Little Lucy or the springs of Dove that one might expect to meet round the bend in the mountain track so much as a bullet through the neck.

6 The economy

Backwardness

To many educated Russians the Empire's economic organisation seemed appallingly backward when comparison was made with the advanced industrial countries of the world. Other nations were forging ahead with industrial progress while Russia still seemed to stagnate under serfdom and its aftermath. Technical skill and capital must clearly be acquired from somewhere if the Empire was to follow in the footsteps of other civilised countries. But was this really desirable? Not all Russians thought so. The slavophiles, for instance, did not believe that western-type progress was suitable for Russia. Still, this was only a minority view, and with the Crimean War even extreme conservatives became impressed by the urgent need to modernise the economy.

Agriculture

The nineteenth century did not see the full transformation of Russia into a modern industrial state. It was with a mainly agricultural economy on a low level of technical development, and with a largely illiterate, primitive and rural population that the Empire ended the century – as she had begun it. In 1900 agriculture remained, as it had been in 1800, the main branch of the Russian economy, at least in the number of people engaged in it. Even by the early twentieth century some three quarters of the population were still engaged in agriculture and the allied pursuits of forestry, fishing and hunting, and it is against this background of a predominant agriculture that the rise of Russian industry must be seen.

Grain was the most important product, though so far as Russian exports are concerned flax and hemp exceeded grain in value until the middle of the 1840s. The largest crop in the north and centre was rye, used mainly for home consumption. But the export trade became dominated by the expanding production of wheat in south Russia, shipped from the Black Sea ports, of which the booming

Odessa was most important. In 1856–60 the grain trade accounted for thirty-five per cent of the overall value of exports, and by the last three decades of the century it had risen even further and came to roughly half (Blum, p. 288; Florinsky, ii, p. 939). Yet these exports formed only a small proportion of the total Russian cereal production, most of which was consumed in Russia itself. Owing to inefficient agricultural methods, yield per acre was low. 'Comparative data collected around the middle of the century revealed that Russian yields were lower than those of any other European nation' (Blum, p. 330).Yet, at the same time, owing to the vast areas available for cultivation, the production of grain per head of population was actually larger than that of any other European country. Other crops – sugar beet, potatoes and grapes for wine – acquired some importance too. But animal husbandry was relatively neglected.

Industry before emancipation

Owing to the institution of serfdom the Russian economy of the early nineteenth century made an antiquated and bizarre impression. Many factories – for example, the metallurgical works and mines of the Urals – were manned chiefly by forced labour. On the other hand cotton manufacture, the most rapidly growing branch of Russian industry in the first half of the nineteenth century, depended largely on hired labour. Hired labourers were free in the sense of not being the serfs of their industrial employer or factory, but this did not mean that they were not serfs. Many had leave of absence from their owners on condition of paying *obrok* (annual money dues). Since textiles were booming while the heavy industry of the Urals stagnated, many Russian employers of the time drew the same conclusion as that often reached by historians later – that forced labour was inefficient. So it was, but this was only one of the factors retarding Russia's economic growth by comparison with that achieved elsewhere. Others included poorer communications over much greater distances.

Commodities could multiply many times in price by the time they had been hauled hundreds or thousands of miles by sledge, boat and rail.

In Russia before 1861 most factory workers were peasants and serfs. They enjoyed much variety in their status and conditions of work. Some worked for no pay on *barshchina* (*corvée*) in factories owned by their masters – distilleries, sugar-beet mills and other 'agricultural' industries in the early years of the century belonging mainly to members of the gentry. Other serfs, notably from the overpopulated and agriculturally poor regions, were, as indicated above, permitted by their owners to hire themselves out, perhaps many days' journey away from their homes, as 'free' labour on condition of paying *obrok*. Others again were possessional serfs attached to a factory and enjoying 'limited serf status', while members of all categories might be skilled or unskilled, part-time or full-time. One surprising feature about these relationships is that an energetic serf could, with the connivance of his owner, become an industrialist and even a millionaire, himself controlling, if not legally possessing, serfs of his own and employing hired labourers.

Cottage industry

An important branch of the economy, which expanded rapidly in the early nineteenth century, was that of cottage industry whereby work was contracted out to be done by peasants in their own homes. The products of such industry might be commissioned by factories, hawked around by pedlars, or sold at one of the great Russian fairs of which those of Nizhny Novgorod and of Irbit in western Siberia were the most celebrated. There was a tendency for the products of the agriculturally poor northern and central provinces to find their way, by an appropriate division of labour, to the richer agricultural land of south Russia, which in turn produced a surplus of grain to feed the poorer provinces. The advancing Russian industrial revolution did not kill the cottage industries, and it has been calculated that at the beginning of the twentieth century some seven or eight million persons were still occupied in them and earning about 500 million roubles a year (Kovalevsky, p. 512).

Industrialisation

Even before 1861 the economy was not stagnant, and the value in roubles of both exports and imports almost tripled between 1826 and 1860. But after the emancipation of the serfs economic development proceeded at a new pace, reaching a particularly high rate of growth in the 1890s. Now the old-fashioned merchant increasingly gave way to the businessman, industrialist and technician, while more antiquated aspects of the economy had yielded to such features of developed capitalism as joint stock companies, stock exchanges and private banks. An industrial labour force of about two hundred thousand in 1800 (exact statistics are not available) had multiplied about fourfold by 1860, and has been calculated at roughly three million all told for the year 1900 (see Seton-Watson, p. 123). Thus serf workmen had given way to a growing industrial proletariat and the themes of labour legislation, trade unions and strikes begin to be heard.

Internal revenue was mainly raised by indirect taxation. Here the excise duty on spirits, merging at the end of the century into a state monopoly of spirits, provided the most productive single item. But as a poor country Russia needed foreign credit to industrialise, and became the largest borrower in Europe.

At first foreign credit was directed chiefly to building railways. Then heavy industry received an impetus from the discovery of iron ore at Krivoy Rog in South Russia and from the development of coal-mining in the Donets Basin two hundred miles to the east. When these two centres were connected by railway in 1884, South Russian industry was thoroughly launched. It in turn fed railway development and also produced armaments, leaving the original heavy industrial centre of the Urals far behind. The main industrial centre in the Donets Basin provides by its changes of name a comment on a whole century of Russian history. It was founded in 1869 as Yuzovka (for Hughesovka) after the Welshman John Hughes, head of the New Russia Metallurgical Company, which set up a metallurgical plant there. In 1924 the name was changed to Stalino, and since Stalin's death it has been changed again – to the more neutral Donetsk, which appeals to local patriotism and carries no offence to political or nationalist sentiment. Another important industrial development took place in the Caucasus with the exploitation of the oil wells at Baku, and of the less productive field at Grozny. During the four years 1898 to 1901 Russia was actually producing more oil than the rest of the world put together.

A crucial part was played in Russia's industrialisation by Sergey Witte, minister of finance from 1892 to 1903. He helped economic development by monetary reform, by encouraging the building of railways, by attracting foreign loans and investments, and also by his policy of tariff protection and of government subsidies and guarantees to Russian industry.

Industrialising late and rapidly on the basis of foreign experience, Russia often had larger-scale and more modern factories than those of western European industrial countries. But alongside these enterprises might be found others extremely primitive. In some important spheres – the electrical and chemical industries, the production of machine-tools – the economy remained particularly weak. On the eve of the first Russian revolution in 1905 it had attained a stature which seemed gigantic if compared with that of the Russian economy of pre-emancipation years. Yet when compared with that of Britain, Germany or the United States, the economy still seemed backward – enormous in potential, but mediocre in realisation.

The coronation of Alexander II in 1856.
A prayer during which His Majesty
alone 'deigns to remain standing'.

7 Emperors

The autocracy

Imperial Russia was an autocracy and its principle of government was accordingly that of absolute power exercised by the monarch. From 1613 until the abdication of Nicholas II and end of the monarchy in February 1917, Russia's rulers came from the house of Romanov and held the official title of Emperor of All Russia, first assumed by Peter the Great. The older title of Tsar, deriving from Latin *Caesar*, also continued to be used.

The Tsar ruled through his personal chancery and through ministers whom he was free to appoint and dismiss at will and whose power might be great, but depended wholly on their standing with him. The ministries and various other governmental bodies (the Senate, the Committee of Ministers, the Council of State, the Council of Ministers) are described below, on pp. 191–2, as is also the Holy Synod, responsible for church affairs (pp. 145–6). Broadly speaking, none of these institutions enjoyed independence or the exercise of initiative except in so far as the Tsar might from time to time decide to heed their advice and except for the Senate's function as a court of appeal.

The profession of Russian Tsar was even more hazardous than that of Russian writer. Three of the last six Tsars met violent deaths, those of Paul (in 1801) and Nicholas II (in 1918) being outside the period covered here. The assassination of Alexander II by revolutionary terrorists in 1881 crowned a whole series of earlier attempts on his life, apart from which there were also rumours, not wholly discounted by historians, that Nicholas I's death in 1855 was due to suicide by poison. Alexander III died naturally, but there had been a plot to murder him too, that of 1887 which led to the execution of Alexander Ulyanov, elder brother of Lenin. In contrast with the lives of relatives cut prematurely short, Alexander I was rumoured to have lived on as a hermit under the alias Fyodor Kuzmich for nearly forty years after his official death in 1825.

One aim of Russian nineteenth-century liberalism was a

Nicholas I (1825–55) Alexander II (1855–81)

constitution limiting the Tsar's absolute powers. After the revolution of 1905 this was achieved to some extent by concessions extracted from Nicholas II, though he did not give up the title of autocrat. But in the period considered here autocratic power was not limited.

Three and a half reigns are involved, as follows: Nicholas I: 1825–55; Alexander II: 1855–81; Alexander III: 1881–94; Nicholas II: 1894–1917 (the last thirteen years being outside the period considered).

Nicholas I and Alexander III were tough, single-minded defenders of the autocratic principle, while Alexander II and Nicholas II were less harsh and uncompromising, so the quartet illustrates a tendency for severe and relatively mild rulers to alternate in Russian history. Alexander II, sometimes called the Tsar-liberator, is associated with the many reforms of the 1860s and 1870s, including the emancipation of the serfs, and Nicholas II granted some constitutional limitations to absolute power, as mentioned above. But neither of them would have thanked historians for calling him a liberal. Each was committed to the autocratic principle, and it happens that each took pains to say so

Alexander III (1881–94)   Nicholas II (1894–1917)

in statements made shortly after accession to the throne. So the nineteenth century was not a period when phases of freedom alternated with phases of oppression in Russia, but one of fluctuating oppression, which was of course never remotely comparable in scope to that practised by the most extreme totalitarian states of the twentieth century.

Nicholas I

Conditions were severest under Nicholas I. The event which began his reign – the unsuccessful Decembrist revolt in St Petersburg in 1825 – helped to set him and his successors on this course, and from 1825 until the abdication of the last Tsar in 1917 fear of revolution haunted Russia's autocrats. Hence the tendency for Russia to support the monarchic principle in Europe and to oppose popular representation at home and abroad. This attitude caused imperial Russia to be identified with nineteenth-century political reaction and to become engaged for example in the suppression of Hungarian revolution in 1849. Hence also the alternation in nineteenth-century Russian history between periods

Count Alexander Benckendorff (1783–1844), Nicholas I's Chief of Gendarmes and Head of the Third Section, was, after the Tsar, the most powerful man in the country. His duties included trying to keep Pushkin in order.

of rigorous repression and attempts to modernise the Russian Empire and turn back the revolutionary tide through reforms which on the whole did too little and came too late.

Such vacillations played no great part in Nicholas I's reign. Even then the idea of reform, including the abolition of serfdom, was reviewed in secret governmental committees, but no effective measures were taken. Impulses towards oppression were received through disturbances within the Empire (the Polish revolt of 1830–1) and outside (the European revolutions of 1830 and 1848–9).

A notable innovation of Nicholas I was the establishment, as part of His Majesty's own chancery, of the so-called Third Section, a special police organisation including a network of secret agents and a uniformed gendarmerie. The first head of the Third Section, from 1826 to 1844, was Count Benckendorff, one of the most powerful figures in the country, responsible to no one save the Emperor himself, and charged, among many other duties, with the regimenting of Pushkin. Like Benckendorff himself, many of Nicholas I's other administrators were generals, and the reign has thus been described as a quasi-military dictatorship by the Tsar.

Nicholas I's policy is most aptly summed up in the slogan Orthodoxy, Autocracy and Nationalism, invented by his Minister of Education, S. S. Uvarov. The last of these three terms, in Russian *narodnost*, is the most elusive, but was once eloquently defined by Benckendorff in a message addressed to Chaadayev, famous for his disparagement of Russian historical achievement: 'Russia's past is admirable; her present more than magnificent; as to her future, it is beyond the grasp of the most daring imagination; this is the point of view . . . from which Russian history must be conceived and written.' Quoting this, the historian Florinsky comments: 'This statement of the Baltic–German nobleman was appropriately delivered in French' (Florinsky, ii, p. 799). He might have added that Benckendorff's master, himself the supreme champion of Russian nationalism, was not very much of a Russian either, for by this time there was little Russian blood in the Romanovs, who were overwhelmingly German by descent.

As well as suppressing the Polish rebellion of 1830–1 and the Hungarian rebellion, in 1849 – both episodes involving large-scale Russian troop movements – Nicholas I also fought three external wars. The first, against Persia in 1826–8, ended with the Treaty of Turkmanchay whereby Russia gained the provinces of Nakhichevan and Erivan. The second, against Turkey in 1828–9, ended with the Treaty of Adrianople whereby Russia made further territorial gains, on the Black Sea coast. The third was the Crimean War of 1853–6, fought against Britain, France and Turkey, and ending in a Russian defeat which the Tsar did not live to witness.

Though Nicholas I began his reign by hanging a poet, and though his last eight years (1848–55) were those of the severest oppression in nineteenth-century Russia, literature flourished during this period. The Russia of Nicholas I was also a period of intense intellectual activity in general, when philosophy, social problems and politics were eagerly discussed, at some risk. But the number of 'conspiracies' unearthed by Nicholas's police was not impressive. The two most important were: the case of the Kiev Brotherhood of Cyril and Methodius, founded in 1846, members of which, including the Ukrainian poet Shevchenko, were arrested in the following year; and the case of the Petrashevsky group, arrested in 1849, in which Dostoyevsky and the poet A. N. Pleshcheyev were implicated.

Military defeat tended to hasten reform in Russia. Such was the effect of Russian reverses in the Crimean War and, later, in the Russo–Japanese War of 1904–5. Each of these operations laid bare such incompetence in the workings of imperial Russia that Russians of all shades of opinion tended to feel that there might be something to be said for tampering with the *status quo*. Coinciding with the death of Nicholas I, defeat in the Crimea thus helped to create a new atmosphere and to usher in the era of reform presided over by Alexander II.

Alexander II

How effective these 'great reforms' were is a matter of dispute and it is generally agreed that the most far-reaching, the emancipation of the serfs in 1861, was no unqualified success. Yet 1861 remains the most important single date in nineteenth-century Russian history. Through emancipation the peasants, the most numerous social class in the community, were raised from a level of near-slavery and became free, or at least freer men. But the main effect of emancipation was moral rather than social or economic. No longer owned by individual landowners, the liberated serfs were left in a state of economic dependence and social inferiority. And they were placed in bondage to their own village communes, where such existed – as they did in most parts of Great Russia. This put severe limitations on their newly-granted freedom. Emancipation was accompanied by widespread peasant disturbances, for many of the ex-serfs felt cheated and expected a second, real emancipation whereby all the land would be turned over to them and the land-owners would be expelled.

The other reforms of Alexander II involved the overhaul of judicial procedure, including the establishment of trial by jury. A new system of local government was instituted with the introduction of provincial and district zemstvos (rural councils) and also of municipal councils. Other important reforms removed some restrictions on schools and universities. Still others turned the army into less of a penal institution, brought in a fairer conscription system and made military punishments less savage. The impact of individual reforms will be discussed more fully in later chapters.

After the stifling atmosphere under Nicholas I, Russians felt themselves able to breathe again under his successor. But various untoward events continued to activate the machinery of oppression, though they did not deter Alexander II from his determination to bring in reforms. They included peasant disturbances at the time of emancipation and a succession of mysterious fires which broke out in St Petersburg in 1862 and were widely attributed to revolutionary arsonists. There was also the Polish insurrection of 1863, which once more brought a large Russian army into Poland, and above all the attempt by a former student, Dmitry Karakozov, to assassinate the Tsar in 1866. Things did not become easier in the 1870s, when intellectuals, mainly students, upset authority by taking part in the movement known as going to the people – invading the Russian villages to educate and agitate the peasantry. The movement was suppressed by the government, and was succeeded by the conspiratorial terrorism which culminated in the assassination of Alexander II in 1881.

In addition to large territorial gains made in Central Asia and the Far East, Alexander II's reign also saw the defeat of Turkey in the war of 1877–8, which ended with the Treaty of San Stefano. By opposing Turkey, Russia emerged as the champion of the Balkan Slavs, and the episode gave a boost to extreme Russian nationalism, which flourished on an official level in the next reign.

Alexander III

As a political manoeuvre the assassination of Alexander II was not a great success from the point of view of the assassins, merely leading to the replacement of a relatively easy-going sovereign by another of tougher fibre. And the revolutionary movement lost momentum in the 1880s. The new Tsar, Alexander III, seemed in many ways a throw-back to his grandfather, Nicholas I. An archconservative, he in effect reinstated the slogan Orthodoxy, Autocracy and Nationalism as the guiding light of policy. Religious and ethnic minorities were persecuted, including the Jews. Thus the 1880s were, as already noted, a time of anti-Jewish pogroms, as also of the imposition of the quota for the admission of Jews to high schools and universities. A series of measures, sometimes termed counter-reforms, involved the imposition of new restrictions on the peasantry, especially by the appointment from among the gentry of newly instituted officials called land captains (*zemskiye nachalniki*) with wide powers. Other measures watered down Alexander II's legal and educational reforms.

In imposing such measures, Alexander III was encouraged by one of his closest advisers, Konstantin Pobedonostsev, who held the post of chief procurator of the Holy Synod of the Russian Orthodox Church from 1880 to 1905 and had been the Tsar's own tutor, as he also was of the Tsarevich, the future Nicholas II. Pobedonostsev, one of the most powerful men of his age, is portrayed as 'Toporov' in Tolstoy's *Resurrection*. He was only the most influential among a group of ultra-conservative advisers, including administrators such as Count D. A. Tolstoy, minister of education and later of internal affairs, and I. N. Durnovo, his successor in the latter post. There were also journalists, notably M. N. Katkov, who supported and encouraged the Tsar in the successful defence of his absolute power. Another pillar of autocracy was Dostoyevsky, in his later years an associate of Pobedonostsev.

The great famine of 1891–2 and the ensuing cholera epidemic were important episodes of Alexander III's reign. Like other disasters of the century, these indirectly encouraged liberal forces, since the government could not cope with the crisis and had to let the zemstvos and other non-governmental bodies help with relief. Tolstoy and Chekhov both took part, Tolstoy helping to organise a large chain of soup-kitchens for the starving peasants, and Chekhov using his expertise as a doctor to direct anti-cholera precautions in an area of twenty-five villages.

A cartoon of Nicholas II and his ministers published in St Petersburg in the revolutionary year 1905. From left to right: Durnovo (Minister of the Interior), Witte (Prime Minister). Pobedonostsev (Procurator of the Holy Synod) and the Tsar, shown as part of a comic band.

Nicholas II

Another calamity, occurring on 18th May 1896 during the celebrations for Nicholas II's coronation (he succeeded Alexander III in 1894), seems in retrospect to cast an aura of impending doom over the ill-starred reign of Russia's last autocrat. This was the death of over a thousand people assembled on the Khodynka Field near Moscow, in a mass stampede which took place as the result of negligence by the authorities, just as they were about to receive traditional presents from the Tsar. A short story by Tolstoy, based on the incident, was published posthumously (*Khodynka*, 1912). On the same evening the Tsar and Tsaritsa tactlessly attended a ball given by the French ambassador, and the whole episode seems to set the scene almost too aptly for the twilight of the Romanovs.

Nicholas II did not intend to be the last Romanov, seeing himself as a defender of the faith and of the autocratic principle, but he was weaker than his father, and more at home as a family man playing with children and dogs than as an arbiter of destiny. His policy in appointing and dismissing ministers was erratic. He was easily influenced by unbalanced or unscrupulous advisers and court favourites, the most notorious being Rasputin, whose sway comes outside the period considered here. Nicholas clung tenaciously to supreme power, but by the late 1890s Russia seemed to be acquiring a political and economic momentum of her own. There was a new spirit of independence which even a less weak-willed autocrat might have failed to quell. As Russia advanced, educationally and industrially, the Tsar and his court began to seem more and more of an anachronism, and Nicholas himself might have been designed by nature to undermine the system which he set himself to prop up. That a ruler so out of touch with the realities of the situation could remain in power for twenty-three years, which included defeat in two major wars, argues more stability in the Russian monarchy than historians have sometimes allowed it.

The really crucial events of Nicholas II's reign fall outside the period considered here, being: the Russo–Japanese War of 1904–5; the first Russian revolution, that of 1905; and above all the First World War, which weakened the structure of imperial Russia to the point where the monarchy collapsed with Nicholas II's abdication at the time of the February revolution of 1917.

PART THREE

The social setting

8 The 'estates'

The Empire's population, both Russian and non-Russian, fell into a number of social categories according to a complicated system. In the first instance the vast majority of the inhabitants could be classed as native subjects. These comprised the entire population (including non-Russians) except for three relatively small groups: foreign nationals resident in Russia; the inhabitants of Finland; and the peoples termed 'those of other race' (*inorodtsy*), consisting of Jews, but also of various primitive tribes.

Among the above the inhabitants of Finland were further sub-divided into social classes according to a separate system which was inherited from Finland's period as a dependency of Sweden and need not be considered here. What must be explained now is the array of social groups into which the native subjects of the Empire, and also the Jews, were subdivided. To one or other of these groups (*sosloviya* or *sostoyaniya*), which may be termed estates, every individual was obliged at least in theory to belong. Each estate had its own special status in law and its own peculiar advantages or obligations.

There was thus no general category of Russian citizen. There were instead the estates of the gentry (hereditary and personal), clergy and peasantry. There were also several groups into which 'town-dwellers' were divided, those of: honorary citizens (hereditary and personal); merchants; craftsmen; and burghers (*meshchane*). But to make matters more complicated, only about half of the actual population of the towns consisted of members of these town-dwellers' estates, the remainder belonging to other estates, chiefly that of the peasantry. The Cossacks too rated as an estate, being divided into gentry and ordinary Cossacks. As is shown by the existence of a Cossack gentry, members of which in a sense belonged to two estates, the borderline between these groups was not always very precise, and membership of one estate need not exclude membership of another. It was customary also to speak of members of the armed forces as belonging to the military estates, though of course many officers were also members of the gentry. Officials were also often spoken of as forming an estate,

St Petersburg types –
a lithograph by
I.S.Shchedrovsky showing
peasant or lower class
urban dress. Many town-
dwellers held the legal
status of peasants.

though some of them belonged to that of the gentry as well.

Closer examination only confirms the unsystematic pattern presented by the Empire's social strata. In certain groups children automatically inherited the social status of their parents, as was the case with the hereditary gentry, hereditary honorary citizens, burghers and peasants. In other groups – those of the merchants, personal gentry and personal honorary citizens – status was not so transmitted. Most groups possessed a corporate organisation – the assemblies of the gentry; the merchants' guilds; the craft corporations; and the burghers' and peasants' communes. But the honorary citizens had no such organisation. Corporate organisations might exist below and up to the level of provinces, as they did in the case of the gentry. In one case there was overall control over a whole estate on an all-Russian level, since the whole clergy came under the supervision of the Holy Synod.

The legal position of the estates changed during the course of the century and the situation became more fluid. Originally the two estates of gentry and clergy were called privileged because their members enjoyed three advantages: freedom from conscription, from corporal punishment and from personal taxation. Hence the other estates were sometimes termed 'taxed'. With the restrictions on corporal punishment enacted in 1863, the introduction of universal liability to conscription in 1874 and the abolition of the poll-tax by 1887, the position changed. But other things being equal it was still worth being a gentleman rather than a member of the other estates. There was, it should be added, a certain amount of mobility between estates. For instance the attainment of sufficiently high military or civil rank automatically conferred entry to the gentry, as might the possession of sufficient funds to the estate of the merchants.

The relative size of the groups may be judged by the following figures showing the membership of the main estates or groups of estates as a percentage of the population at the end of the nineteenth century (from Kovalevsky, p. 67):

Peasants	81·5 per cent
'Town-dwellers'	9 per cent
Military estates	6·5 per cent
Gentry	just over 1 per cent
Clergy	just under 1 per cent

The position of individual social groups is discussed in greater detail below.

9 Peasants

General situation

The estate of the peasantry accounted for an overwhelming majority of the Empire's inhabitants, about four out of every five persons, who were in many ways a class apart, as they remain to some extent even nowadays. Peasants of the nineteenth century spoke, as they speak today, a Russian more earthy and vivid than that of the intellectual, but surprisingly uniform within the Great Russian area if comparison is made with the variety of dialects that exist in such countries as Germany and Italy. Most peasants were illiterate. Even as late as 1897 census data showed that only twenty-two per cent of the rural population between the ages of 9 and 49 could read and write (Utechin, *Encyclopaedia*, p. 225).

The peasants were often said to carry the Empire on their backs. Even after emancipation they were still far from free, and they bore an excessive share of the tax burden. Their housing, clothing and food were of wretched quality. They were generally devoted to the Tsar, in popular mythology a benevolent figure misled by evil officials who stood between him and his subjects.

The peasants were given to extremes of kindness and cruelty. They were apt to riot, looting the local manor-house, murdering the squire and his family, and letting loose 'the red cock' by setting fire to his property. They were regular church-goers who kept the strict prescribed fasts, but were also punctilious in performing the ritual of wife-beating. Bullied and patronised in turn by the privileged classes of Russia, to whom they seemed a sinister enigma, but also the repository of some mysterious virtue defying analysis, they were designated by the potent emotional word *narod*, which can also mean 'people' or 'nation'. They also had the habit of calling themselves 'dark people' (*tyomnyye lyudi*).

Some peasants in literature

Russian literature has much to say about peasant life, one of the best-known works concerned being Gogol's *Dead Souls*. Actual peasant characters play small part in it, but an eloquent comment on serfdom is made by the hero's attempt to buy up and mortgage 'dead souls', these being male serfs who had expired since the previous census was taken, but remained subject to tax until the next one. The emerging realist movement burst on the Russian reading public with a number of works about the Russian peasantry, of which Turgenev's *Sportsman's Sketches* are the best known. Grigorovich's stories *The Village* and *Poor Anton* were other influential portrayals of serfs. Among later descriptions of the peasant, those of Tolstoy and Chekhov are major contributions from fiction-writers of the front rank, Chekhov's story *Peasants* (1897) containing an especially good short description of Russian village life. Other writers who treated the theme include some associated with the populist movement of the late nineteenth century, such as Gleb Uspensky and Alexander Ertel (see below, p. 244). Nor was the peasant neglected in poetry, Aleksey Koltsov, Ivan Nikitin and – in his very different way – Nekrasov being among those who used peasant idiom in verse. Nekrasov's long narrative poem *Who Can Be Happy in Russia?* contains some lively passages, but the miseries which it describes and its mournful title set the tone for much of Russian peasant literature. This is apt to be sad, but so after all was the peasant's life.

Serfs

Since the institution of serfdom existed during a large part of the period considered here, some comments on the status of the peasants during that time are required. There were about fifty million peasants in all at the time of emancipation. Of these slightly less than half were serfs in the sense of belonging to landowning masters. The word serf is also sometimes loosely applied to the large class of state peasants who lived on property owned and administered by the state and outnumbered the serfs proper at the time of emancipation (Blum, pp. 476–7). There were other categories too, including the 'appanage' peasants who lived on properties belonging to the imperial court. It was the landowner's serfs who on the whole suffered the worst conditions – especially those of them who were taken into the squire's house as domestic servants (*dvorovyye lyudi*) – always under the master's eye and eventually emancipated without land. This did not stop some of them from hankering, like Firs in Chekhov's *Cherry Orchard*, after the good old days before the Troubles – Firs's word for the emancipation.

Some of the serf's troubles arose from the system called *barshchina* (*corvée*), whereby three days' unpaid labour a week was due to the squire, and more might easily be exacted. For despite feeble attempts by the government to limit the worst abuses of the serf system, landowners could in practice do as they liked with their serfs – mortgage them, separate them from their families, lose them at cards, pack them off into the army for twenty-five years or have them flogged. The more kind-hearted landlord might grant his peasants some relief by changing the *barshchina* system for that of an annual money-due (*obrok*), as did Eugene Onegin in Pushkin's verse novel, who (to give a rather unpoetical translation) 'substituted an easy *obrok* for the yoke of burdensome *barshchina*' on his newly inherited estate. As the *obrok* system reminds one, peasants were by no means shackled to the soil. Provided that they paid the required dues, they were permitted, indeed encouraged, to go and get a job, perhaps many hundreds of miles away from home. They might, as shown above, become part-time or full-time factory workers, and it was as a result of this system that a large proportion of the urban population of Russia consisted of peasants (for the landlord-serf relationship, see further pp. 140–1 below).

Dwellings

Both before and after emancipation Russian villages and the peasant huts of which they were largely composed, made a dreary impression. This was partly due to the uniformity of the buildings and of the layout of the villages, at least in Great Russia, with which the present description is concerned. It was not normal, as it is in many countries, to have isolated peasant holdings. Huts were usually crowded close together, each standing on an oblong plot of land. Thus a typical small village was just two rows of huts separated by the 'road' – a broad, unpaved strip which, depending on the weather, consisted of mud, slush, dust or snow. Larger villages would be diversified by side-roads running at right angles, and some relief to the eye might be supplied by the outline of a village church, especially if this had brightly-painted onion-domes. Otherwise the village huts all tended to look alike within a given area, though there were variations in style from one part of the country to another.

Wood was the main building material. The walls were of logs laid horizontally on top of one another, the cracks being stuffed with moss or tow, and the wood round windows and doorways often being elaborately carved. Size varied according to the availability of manpower and timber. In northern villages, where

severer winter weather was often combined with dense forests in the neighbourhood, huts were larger. They might run to two storeys, apart from which they would have a fairly roomy 'cellar' (*podklet*) obtained by setting the floor five to ten feet above the ground at the level between the sixth and tenth beam up. Hence the characteristic height of the living-room windows in a Russian hut when viewed from street level. The cellar was used for hens, for the young of domestic animals and for general storage purposes. Further to the south, shortage of timber made it necessary to economise on the height of the cellar and on size generally. It also brought an important structural variation – the use of straw thatch instead of wood as roofing material.

Peasants usually built their own huts, often being as handy with their axes as they were with scythe and sickle. Three men working hard could knock up a typical hut in a matter of weeks, and the modest outbuildings took even less time. As this illustrates, the peasants tended to be economically self-sufficient, and the women were at least as adept with loom and spindle as the men with their axes. Thus the peasants' was largely a subsistence economy. They made their own huts, clothes and agricultural gear, and used little money – though the use of money was in fact on the increase.

The most important part of the peasant homestead was the heated living-room. It served as a drawing-room, dining-room, kitchen and bedroom combined for the whole family, which might easily include three generations. The most important inanimate object was a huge stove of brick or rammed clay, occupying a sixth or more of the total area. After about 1880 it became customary to equip stoves with chimneys, but in earlier huts so-called 'black' heating was the rule. This meant that the stove simply spouted its smoke straight into the living-room, an ordeal to the uninitiated. But the Russian peasant was used to it, having been rocked and (one is tempted to add) kippered in a cradle near the ceiling, where smoke was thickest, in his earliest years.

As a visitor entered a typical living-room the stove might be on the right of the door as he went in, and he would find himself

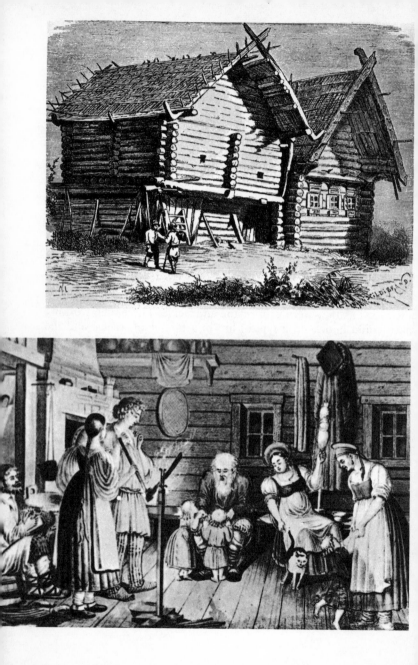

facing the wall which gave on to the street and had three small windows, probably not more than two foot high and not much more than one foot wide. Another similar window, to the left, might look out on the yard. On the left corner (the so-called 'red' or 'front' corner) of the wall facing the road there would be a shelf or case containing an icon with a lamp burning in front of it, and every peasant who entered the hut would face this and cross himself before doing anything else.

There would not normally be beds or chairs, the functions of both being fulfilled by wooden benches running along the walls. Peasants usually slept in or under their daytime clothes. In addition to the benches a structure known as the *polati* – being removable boards set on posts at about the height of the top of the stove and

usually placed against the wall facing the windows – provided, together with the stove itself, a convenient sleeping platform. This eminence was also a place for stowing dotards and children, being a vantage-point from which they could watch domestic dramas unfolding below them. A crude table, a cupboard containing half a dozen bowls, wooden spoons, a few knives, dishes, pots and other utensils, a washing-tub – these would almost complete the simple inventory, except for the pictures, perhaps just cut out of magazines and pasted on the wall. They might portray the Russian Imperial Family, biblical scenes, the battles of Inkerman or Alma, St George and the Dragon or episodes from Russian folk-lore. One important and much-prized item might also be found. This was the samovar for boiling water with which to make tea – a favourite peasant drink, but a luxury.

In a country where the neglectful froze to death in winter the stove was a vital item. Besides warmth it provided a means of baking bread and cooking. And it was often possible to take a steam-bath inside the huge oven, as was common in the south. In the north, where more wood was available and the influence of the Finnish sauna may be suspected, a peasant household would have its own bath-house – a small, crude hut with a stove, set away from the main hut. The peasants' steam-bath on Saturday nights was an important part of their weekly ritual, and it is quite true that they enjoyed a roll in the snow after steaming themselves and lashing themselves with birch switches.

Matches and paraffin-lamps were luxuries which were becoming available at the end of the century, but peasants who lacked them had to preserve fire by banking down the stove at night and blowing on it to revive it in the morning. Before the days of paraffin-lamps, burning strips of wood (*luchiny*), set on a special stand, supplied a meagre, smoky light. Clumsily managed stoves would disgorge poisonous fumes (*ugar*) into the hut, whence the idiom 'to thrash around like an *ugorely*' (one who has been subjected to carbon monoxide fumes from a Russian stove).

So much for the typical living-room. It did not usually have an outside door, but was approached through a sort of entrance-lobby called the *seni*. On the other side of this from the living-room might be a storeroom (*klet*) – unheated, but used in summer as an overflow living-room. To enter his yard from the main living-room the peasant might turn right after stepping into the lobby and go out through a porch. He might then find, on his right, a high wooden fence, continuing the line of the front of the hut, and containing a small door and also a large gate giving on to the road. Opposite him might be his carts, sledges, ploughs and other impedimenta, stowed in the open under the overhanging roof of the shed which housed any horses, cows and sheep. There might be a pig-shed adjoining it, and round at the back might be grain-store, threshing-barn and kitchen-garden.

Such, with many local variations, was the dwelling that Russian peasants built anywhere in the Empire where timber was available. Wood supplied shelter and fuel. But in the treeless steppe of the south, huts were heated with dried dung and were made of rammed clay or wattle. They were whitewashed, stood in their own gardens, and were scattered about in disregard of the rectilinear principles practised in the forests. They were also normally known by a different name (*khata* instead of *izba*) and might present a more cheery spectacle, at least in the Ukraine. But the huts of southern Great Russia were particularly wretched.

The miseries of the peasantry were increased by the constant danger of fire in the Russian village, so that the Russian language even has a special word – *pogorelets* – to describe someone rendered homeless and destitute by having his hut burnt down. Fire too inspired a common Russian proverb: 'My hut's on the end' (i.e. at the opposite end of the village to the fire), this being the equivalent of the English 'I'm all right, Jack'. Chekhov's *Peasants* contains a good short description of a fire which occurred through carelessness with a samovar and was happily put out, before much damage was done, by a young squire of the locality, helped by women hauling water from the river and surrounded by less helpful drunken muzhiks who staggered out of the village inn.

Marriage

The peasants' attitude to their womenfolk was rarely chivalrous or sentimental. A wife, like a horse, was a necessary beast of burden. So marriages were commonly planned with an eye to economic advantage, being arranged by the young people's parents. However, love matches – sometimes by elopement followed by a plea for the parents' forgiveness – were by no means unknown, and they became more common towards the end of the period. Peasants usually married young, the girls at sixteen to eighteen years old and the men at a year or two older.

Peasant marriage was associated with traditional rituals so complex – and with so many local variations – that there is not space to describe them in detail. They began with the ceremony of matchmaking whereby a team of negotiators (perhaps consisting of the young man's uncle or elder brother with wives, godparents and other interested parties) set out at night – to avoid detection – for the home of some marriageable girl. On receiving a favourable response from her parents a further meeting would be arranged to discuss such matters as the dowry and the financial contribution to be made by the groom's family to the wedding. In some areas this discussion bore a name which one is tempted to translate 'the little booze-up' (*maly zapoy*). It was followed later by the 'big booze-up', in effect a betrothal ceremony after which neither side could honourably withdraw.

On the wedding eve bride and groom held separate farewell parties for their friends of the same sex. The bride also took a steam-bath on that day or on the wedding day itself, when she was dressed by her girl friends. The groom went in procession with his best man and various assistants to the bride's home where a number of ceremonies might be performed including the symbolic purchase of the bride. After the wedding ceremony bride and groom were led to the nuptial couch by the chief female matchmaker (*svakha*) and best man (*druzhka*), and it was the bride's first duty to remove her husband's boots as a sign of submissiveness. Next morning the matchmaker and best man would waken the couple and display the bride's smock in a condition reputedly bearing evidence as to her virginity before marriage.

It was not uncommon for the wedding festivities themselves to last up to six days, quite apart from various follow-up ceremonies which ensued during the next weeks and months. But by the end of the century these practices were being generally simplified and shortened.

Children

A high birth rate and a high rate of infant mortality were character-istic of peasant families, so that Marya (in Chekhov's *Peasants*) who 'had thirteen children, of whom only six had lived' was by no means exceptional. Though Russian peasant women are famous for giving birth in the fields at harvest time, babies were more commonly delivered by a peasant midwife (*povitukha*) on the shelf in the family bath-hut – which, it will be remembered, was a small structure separate from the main peasant hut. This was thought to protect the main hut from the pollution supposedly associated with childbirth and the newly born baby from the danger of the evil eye. The mother might well be working in the fields a week later. Christening usually followed a day or two after birth. The baby was commonly slung from the ceiling of the hut in a cradle and was breast-fed up to the age of a year or eighteen months. The practice of wrapping Russian babies in tight swaddling clothes, from which they are periodically released for a delicious feed and romp, has been invoked as an explanation of the Russian national character – allegedly prone to switch between extremes of gloom and gaiety, sloth and wild activity.

Peasant children had a hard life. They were often beaten, were expected to be subservient to their elders and were required to work at family chores (weaving for the girls, farm-work for the boys) from the earliest possible age. In certain areas they might be despatched to town at about the age of twelve or thirteen, the girls to do domestic service and the boys to be apprentice waiters, cobblers, bakers and so on.

Funerals

The body of a dead peasant would be laid out on a bench in the 'red' corner of the hut (that containing the icon), with his head towards the icon. The body would be carried to the funeral in an open coffin and after the ceremony it was customary to hold a 'wake' (*pominki*) – not always as uproarious an affair as that which follows the obsequies of Marmeladov in Dostoyevsky's *Crime and Punishment*.

Drinking habits

The typical village inn was just another hut which might be a bit bigger than its neighbours. It would even house the usual icon with lamp burning in front of it, as found in any peasant's hut. 'The floor is dirty,' according to one description of a typical inn, dated 1898 (Isayev, p. 40) 'and so are both walls and tables. Even dirtier are the red cotton table-cloths with which they are covered in some places. The lamp, which dimly illuminates the pub, is dirty, the glasses and crockery are dirty. There is dust everywhere.' Still, the customers are not fussy, the same observer points out, and gives an almost idyllic picture of the village inn. It may be humble with its bar at one end of the room, holding a couple of bottles of vodka, half a dozen of beer, some salted gherkins and hunks of rye bread on small plates. But it is the social hub of the village, serving as a sort of club, where gossip can be exchanged or commercial deals concluded in congenial surroundings, and where old soldiers can re-live the Turkish campaign of 1877–8 and their memories of the siege of Plevna. It also served as a reading-room and as a place where some village 'scholar' might regale his illiterate fellow-peasants with extracts from a tattered newspaper. Local politics too were discussed – such topics as whether old Yegor would make a good village elder or whether some local official had been dipping his hand in the community till.

Disappointingly, at least to those who would conceive the

Russian village inn as a den of vice, the favourite drink was tea, served in the pot or – for a large group of customers – by the samovar. It was customary to drink glass after glass of tea, getting red in the face until according to Russian idiom it brought out your seventh sweat. For this reason it was sometimes possible to order 'tea, sugar and a towel'.

Not that the Russian peasant neglected alcohol. But surprisingly enough, considering his reputation as a hard drinker, the *per capita* consumption of alcohol throughout the largely peasant Empire was strikingly low compared with that in France, Britain, Germany and Denmark (Schlesinger, p. 14; Bruford, p. 46). The point here is that the Russian peasant was a selective drinker, who confined his drinking to special occasions. There was no lack of these. 'According to an established custom, sanctified by time and by tradition [as is claimed in an official report of 1903] not one event in the social life of the community (such, for example, as the cutting of the hay, or the celebration of the local saint's day), can be gotten through without the drinking of *vodka*; and in just the same way *vodka* is indispensable on very important occasions in the life of the family: at birth, marriages, funeral-feasts, the leave-taking of recruits, and the like' (quoted in Robinson, p. 259).

Besides, when the Russian peasant did drink, he tended to make a thorough job of it. The account in Chekhov's *Peasants* of the goings-on in the village of Zhukovo well conveys the atmosphere of such village orgies:

On Elijah's Day they drank. On the Feast of the Assumption they drank. On Holy Cross Day they drank. The Feast of the Intercession was the parish holiday for Zhukovo and the villagers seized the chance to drink for three days. They drank their way through fifty roubles of communal funds and then the village had a whip-round for more vodka. The Chikildeyevs killed a sheep on the first day and ate vast helpings of it morning, noon and night, and even then the children got up at night for a bite. Kiryak was terribly drunk on all three days. He drank the cap off his head and the boots off his feet, and beat Marya so hard that she had to be doused with water. Later on everyone felt ashamed and sick.

Festivals

As the above extract illustrates, the Russian peasant reckoned his dates by the Orthodox Church calendar and not by months and days. The following table contains the main fixed festivals celebrated by the peasantry, the dates being those of the Julian Calendar (used in Russia until 1918) which, as has been said, lagged behind the Gregorian Calendar (used in western Europe) by twelve days in the nineteenth century and by thirteen days in the twentieth century.

6 January	Epiphany
2 February	*Sreteniye* (The Meeting)
25 March	Annunciation
9 May	St Nicholas's Day (summer)
29 June	St Peter and St Paul's Day
6 August	Transfiguration
15 August	Assumption, Dormition
29 August	The Decapitation of St John the Baptist
8 September	Nativity of the Virgin
14 September	Holy Cross Day
26 September	Death of St John the Apostle
1 October	Intercession of the Virgin
22 October	Our Lady of Kazan
21 November	Presentation of Our Lady
6 December	St Nicholas's Day (winter)
25–27 December	Christmas

To the above, three movable feasts must be added: Easter (the most important of all); Ascension (forty days after Easter); and Whitsun (ten days after Ascension Day), as well as Shrovetide or Carnival preceding Lent.

Fasts

In contrast with these junketings were the severe fasts practised on almost half the days of the year, when the consumption of meat, milk, butter and eggs was forbidden. In each week Wednesday (the day on which Judas betrayed Christ) as well as the more familiar Friday, was a fast day. And there were four more or less prolonged fasts in addition to this: Lent; St Peter's Fast (lasting five weeks and ending on 29th June, the Day of St Peter and St Paul); the Fast of the Assumption (two weeks before 15th August); and the Christmas Fast (six weeks ending on 24th December). A tendency sometimes noted in Russian peasants to swing from the extreme of self-indulgence to the extreme of mortification of the flesh was thus encouraged and sanctified by the Orthodox Church calendar. But since they were often desperately poor, it would be fair to emphasise the element of mortification over that of self-indulgence. With the wealthier classes, especially merchants, it might be the other way round, but peasants took their fasts seriously, often with bad effects on their health. It may be noted that the fasts of St Peter and of the Assumption took place when field work was at its height.

Diet

The staple diet of the peasantry was a simple one: mainly black (rye) bread, supplemented by buckwheat gruel, potatoes, cabbage, cucumber and onions. To the luxuries of tea and vodka, mentioned above, must be added the more humdrum national drink – kvass made from fermented black bread. Meat was a rare luxury, and there was little milk.

Dress

The poorer peasants' working clothes tended to be simple home-made articles. In summer they might go barefoot or would wear bast shoes (*lapti*), while felt boots (*valenki*) supplied protection against the cold of winter. They wore trousers, linen shirts and various styles of coat or tunic, including the caftan and *poddyovka*. Overcoats of sheepskin were worn in winter, with a sort of super-

Ploughing with the traditional wooden plough (*sokha*). The *sokha* was light and wheelless and did not cut deep enough to be really effective. Some enterprising landowners tried to modernise Russian agriculture, but the peasants tended to be conservative and highly suspicious of new-fangled methods and implements.

topcoat (*tulup*), also usually of sheepskin and bound round with a coloured cummerbund, to go on top of that for travelling purposes. (One must remember that Russians travelled in open sleighs.) In descriptions of winter in Russian literature, there is a close association between peasants and the smell of sheepskins.

Peasants tried to keep more elaborate clothes in reserve for holidays, when the better-off young men might wear baggy velveteen trousers (*sharovary*). Resplendent in bright shirts made of bought material, the young dandies of the village sometimes sported a single silver ear-ring. Great importance was attached to the possession of highly polished top-boots, into which trousers were tucked, and which were so prized that young men sometimes took them off when they had to walk through mud.

Peasants, especially before the emancipation, did not shave their beards. The most characteristic hat was a felt affair shaped something like a top-hat, and they had fur caps, preferably with ear-flaps, for winter wear.

The clothes of peasant women offered much greater variety, but with the same tendency to keep special dresses for holidays. The most characteristic item was the *sarafan*, a sort of sleeveless slip. On holidays elaborately embroidered or ornamented clothes might be worn, including the *kokoshnik*, a kind of head-dress adorned

with artificial pearls in place of the humble but gaudy kerchief worn on ordinary working days.

Peasant farming

St George's Day (23rd April) was considered the beginning of work in the fields in many parts, and until early June the sowing of spring corn would be the chief occupation. The second half of June was devoted to ploughing for winter corn. With the arrival of St Peter and St Paul's Day on 29th June came the beginning of haymaking, the province of the men of the village who would use scythes. Reaping was done by sickle in Great Russia, and this work, in which both men and women joined, was reckoned the hardest of all. By tradition Elijah's Day (20th July) marked the beginning and Assumption (15th August) the end of the harvest. With the gathering of the spring-sown corn and the sowing of the winter corn for the following year, the exhausting but short agricultural cycle of under six months was finished. By 1st October, the Feast of the Intercession, the peasant was back in his hut with nothing but the threshing between him and his winter occupations. These might involve mending and making agricultural implements, work of cottage industry type in his own home, non-agricultural seasonal work in some town not necessarily very near by – or, according to age, temperament and resources, simply lazing on the stove.

Physically active as the Russian peasant had been during his five or six months in the fields, he was not among the more efficient farmers of Europe. This was due less to lack of strength and intelligence than to other causes. Primitive methods and primitive implements were still in use at the end of the century. The traditional light, wheelless plough called *sokha* was still being widely employed, though it cut too shallow a furrow. The three-field system of cropping, the most common technique, involved putting one field down to winter corn and another to spring corn, while a third was left fallow, the crops being then rotated. A peasant household would hold a narrow strip in each of the three fields, and often several strips in each field, the different strips being frequently far separated both from each other and from the cultivator's hut, with consequent waste of time in getting from one to the other. The narrowness of the strips, sometimes as little as two yards across, precluded cross-ploughing and resulted in land going to waste on providing boundaries.

Then again, individual farmers were discouraged from improving their land because of the communal system of land-tenure, according to which, in most of the Great Russian area of European Russia, the arable land was liable to repartition every so often. Manure was in short supply owing to the neglect of animal husbandry, and why bother to manure or clear land when you were going to lose it anyway just as soon as the next repartition occurred? Then there were the unsuitable soil and climatic conditions – the bogs and infertile soils of central Russia and the insufficient rainfall of the black earth region, immensely fertile as it was in potential. The difficulty of transporting produce owing to poor communications was another handicap.

To the above must be added the traditional 'go-slow' attitude bred in the peasants by centuries of oppression. Their attitude to the squire, who owned the peasants themselves along with the land before emancipation, was one of deep suspicion which continued long after the peasants had become free men and had perhaps begun to work for the local landowner as hired labourers. Well-meaning landowners might sincerely propose generous innovations of benefit to the peasantry, as did Levin, in *Anna Karenin*, Nekhlyudov in *Resurrection* and many other Tolstoyan heroes, but the peasants remained stubbornly convinced that there must be some snag even if they could not see what it was. This attitude made things difficult for those landlords who wished to improve farming methods by mechanisation. The peasants often refused to use the new machinery, and would break it, accidentally or on purpose.

Communes

After emancipation mere removal – even if permanent residence was involved – to a town, did not mean that a villager lost the legal status of peasant. By one of the provisions of emancipation, peasants belonging to a village commune remained attached to their commune, which now took over some of the original serf-owners' claims on individuals.

A few words must be said about this much-discussed institution of the Russian village commune, known in Russia as *obshchestvo* ('society') and sometimes as *obshchina* or *mir*. It is its composition and functions which are of concern in the present study rather than its highly controversial origins. The village contained a number of households, consisting normally of a single family inhabiting a single dwelling. A household might well include numerous daughters-in-law and grandchildren, though after emancipation there was a tendency for such large joint-families to split up. One person, normally the oldest non-senile male, was head of the household, and the governing body of the commune consisted of a meeting of all these heads of households. Not all were men, for a widowed woman might attend and speak at the gathering if she happened to be the head of her household.

The meetings of heads of household usually took place on holidays or Sundays in the open air amid lively discussion by members no less articulate for being mostly illiterate. By a curious tradition it came about that decisions of the assembly were usually unanimous. One duty of the assembly was to elect a village elder (*starosta*) for a period of three years. The elder's was a thankless job and not much sought after. He presided over meetings, and was responsible for collecting the tax imposed on the commune as a whole. He might, like the officious Antip Sedelnikov in Chekhov's *Peasants*, confiscate the samovar of an offending household as a means of forcing the payment of arrears, or even lock up an old woman for swearing at a village meeting. On a less grotesque level, he was also responsible for the call-up of peasants into the forces, had the duty of reporting suspicious strangers to the police and could arrest criminals. He wore a bronze medallion on a chain round his neck as a badge of office.

No peasant could leave his own area without a passport, and a passport could not be granted without permission of the head of household (unless the applicant were himself head of a household) and also of the village assembly. Hence the claim made by some historians that after emancipation the peasant exchanged bondage to a landowner for bondage to the commune. Even if he got his passport, he still retained membership of the commune, with tax responsibilities, whether he liked it or not. Another function of the commune was to allot strips of land to individual households at the time of the periodical redistributions.

Cantons

For administrative convenience communes were grouped together at the time of the emancipation in larger newly established units called cantons (*volosti*). A typical canton was a collection of small villages. It too had its elder (*volostnoy starshina*) as well as a clerk who might perhaps be one of the few persons on the cantonal administration able to read and write, so that he sometimes had more power than was intended. The canton assembly itself, which elected the cantonal elder and other officials, consisted of the elders of the component villages and one representative from each ten households. Apart from its administrative responsibilities, the canton was responsible for forming a court to try minor cases involving peasants, and this was the only judicial organ which retained the right to award corporal punishment after 1863. Members of the gentry holding property within the boundaries of a given canton were, it need hardly be said, not themselves subject to cantonal authority. Nor were professional persons such as doctors and schoolteachers.

In 1889, as part of Alexander III's 'counter-reforms', the powers of the canton were limited by the appointment of newly instituted officials with the title of land captain (*zemsky nachalnik*). It was laid down that these should be drawn wherever possible from the local hereditary landed gentry, and they were given wide discretionary powers. They could arrest or suspend peasant officials and impose fines without trial. But Florinsky probably goes too far when he claims that 'a sham of self-government was preserved, yet peasant Russia was actually ruled by petty officials drawn from the midst of the landed nobility and controlled by the minister of the interior' (Florinsky, ii, p. 1095). On the other hand, Mackenzie Wallace, admittedly writing before the institution of land captains, had gone altogether too far in the opposite direction by calling village communes 'capital specimens of representative Constitutional government of the extreme democratic type' (Mackenzie Wallace, i, pp. 192–3). The truth lay somewhere between these statements.

10 Landowners and gentlemen

Status and organisation

The gentry's importance in Russian culture is completely out of proportion to its numbers – just over one per cent of the population at the end of the nineteenth century. Much Russian literature was written by landowners for landowners about landowners, and by the time of Turgenev the squire's country seat, such as the 'nest of gentlefolk' in the title of one of his novels, had become an established setting for Russian fiction.

Two overlapping concepts are involved here, those of landowner (*pomeshchik*) and gentleman (*dvoryanin*), the latter term denoting membership of one of the estates into which society was divided. It is sometimes rendered 'nobility', so that Turgenev's novel may be alluded to as *A Nest Of Noblemen*, but since the English word nobility implies possession of a title, the less misleading term gentry is preferred here.

Before 1861 a provision (sometimes circumvented, like all Russian provisions) existed whereby no one except a gentleman could own serfs, and as land tenure was usually combined with serf-ownership, a large landowner at the time of serfdom was almost inevitably a member of the gentry class. After emancipation there was a continual decrease in the amount of land held by the gentry, whose holdings passed more and more to members of other classes. Thus Chekhov's *Cherry Orchard*, in which Lopakhin, the self-made son of a former serf, buys a vast estate from feckless genteel owners, seems to sum up over a hundred years of decline from the late eighteenth century under Catherine the Great, the gentry's golden age.

The estate of the gentry could be entered by non-gentlemen who attained high rank in the civil service or armed forces. Though the actual rank giving this right varied according to the regulations currently in force, the important point is that the estate was not exclusive, as some of its members would have liked to make it. Certain civil and military awards – those of St Vladimir and St George, as also the first class of other decorations – likewise conveyed the status of hereditary membership of the gentry. An inferior grade of gentry was that conferred by the status of personal, as opposed to hereditary, gentleman. Personal status was conferred by lower rank than that which gave hereditary gentry status, and, as the title implies, did not devolve to children.

The emperors tended to look to the gentry to resist revolution and support the *status quo*. One of Nicholas I's police chiefs, Dubelt, summed up the position as follows: 'The landowner is the most reliable bulwark of the sovereign. . . . If his power is destroyed, the people will become a flood, endangering in time even the Tsar himself. . . . The landlord is the most faithful, the unsleeping watchdog of the state; he is the natural police-magistrate' (quoted in Sumner, p. 142). The landowners' privileges were intended to preserve their loyalty and encourage them in the performance of specific services. Themselves exempt from flogging, conscription and personal taxation during the period when these inconveniences remained in force, they were responsible under serfdom for collecting poll-tax paid by their peasants, for drafting them into the army and for administering local justice – functions which all passed to the village commune or to the canton after 1861.

The gentry had an elaborate corporate organisation, including gentry assemblies at provincial and district level, presided over by marshals of the gentry who were chosen through a combination of election by their peers with appointment by the ministry of the interior. One of their duties was to see that delinquent gentlemen toed the line. Thus in Chekhov's story *My Life* (1896) the provincial marshal of the gentry reports the hero, Misail Poloznev, to the governor of the province for working as a labourer – conduct unbecoming in a gentleman and son of the local architect.

After the local government reforms of 1864, the marshals of the gentry became *ex officio* chairmen of the assemblies of the newly instituted rural councils, the zemstvos. The institution of land captains appointed from among the gentry in 1889 (see above, p. 131) was another provision whereby the landowning gentry regained some of the control over peasant affairs lost at the time of emancipation.

Titles

The Russians had a titled nobility or aristocracy, but it formed only a small section of the gentry as a whole. Their oldest hereditary title was that of prince (*knyaz*), and many Russian princes traced their descent from the semi-legendary founder of the Russian state, Ryurik, said to have died in 879 AD. Others were descendants of Gedimin, Prince of Lithuania, or of Tatar or Georgian princes. Members of the Tsar's family held the title *veliky knyaz* (literally 'great prince'), for which grand duke is used in English. Prince was the only Russian title in use in the nineteenth century that dated from before Peter the Great, who introduced new grades of nobility: those of count (*graf*) and baron. The latter title was held by many members of the German nobility in the Russian Baltic, who so often reached high rank in the administration. When awarded to Russians it came to be granted to successful businessmen, so that princes and counts somewhat looked down on it.

By contrast with French and English practice, titles were inherited by all the children of a titled father, whence the large number of princes, princesses, counts and countesses scattered through the pages of Russian novels. It was also usual for property to be split among all the sons of a family, not left exclusively to an eldest son – hence a tendency for members of the aristocracy to be poorer than their rank suggests. There was thus nothing improbable in Dostoyevsky beginning his *Idiot* by introducing a penniless Prince Myshkin almost in the role of beggar and suppliant, while if the name of a Prince Golitsyn cropped up in real life, the question was apt to be asked: 'Who is this Golitsyn? A rich one or a poor one?' (Blum, p. 376).

Dress

Peter the Great had compelled the gentry to dress like western Europeans by wearing what the peasants called 'German clothes', whereas clergy, merchants and peasants continued wearing traditional Russian dress. In the nineteenth century this differentiation by dress was maintained. Thus the heroine of Pushkin's *Young Lady as Peasant*, one of his *Tales of Belkin*, was able to pass herself off as a peasant girl only after getting her maids to run her up a rustic shirt and *sarafan* specially for the occasion. While remaining distinct from the clothing of other classes, the dress of the gentry did of course change according to changes in fashion. For ladies it was full skirts in the thirties and crinolines in the sixties. At the beginning of the nineteenth century men were wearing tail-coats. These continued to be formal wear, but were ousted for more ordinary occasions by frock-coats and later by jackets and dinner-jackets, as were top hats by bowlers. Waistcoats were considered essential wear for a gentleman. By the end of the nineteenth century, distinction of dress was becoming less marked in the sense that gentry and non-gentry townspeople were dressing more and more alike.

Use of French

As readers of Tolstoy's *War and Peace* will remember, French was a common means of communication for the Russian gentry at the beginning of the nineteenth century – in fact there were many Russian gentlemen who spoke it better than their own language. In a way Pushkin knew Russian better than anyone else before or since, but he regularly wrote to his Russian wife in French. Herzen explains that his father wrote better French than Russian and would never so much as read a Russian book. He did once take up Karamzin's *History of the Russian State*, hearing that Alexander I had read it, but soon laid it down, saying: 'All these Izyaslaviches and Olgoviches – what a bore!' (*My Past and Thoughts*, ch. v). After the discovery of Anna Karenin's adultery, her husband found it convenient to speak to her in French, for *vous* seemed chilly enough to express his disapproval, whereas the polite second person plural would have meant too harsh a transition from the

A gentleman, Count Ya. I. Rostovtsev, and his family, from
a painting by S. Zaryanko, 1904. The social 'estate' of the
gentry accounted for about one per cent of the population.
It dominated Russian culture, though its power and influence steadily
declined as other social groups increasingly competed. Even the
revolutionary movement was largely a dispute between gentlemen.

intimate form *ty*. As for Dostoyevsky, being a rabid Russian nationalist he objected to the practice of bringing up genteel infants to speak French: 'Mummy doesn't know with what venom she is poisoning her child as early as the age of two, when she invites a French *bonne* to look after him' (*Diary of a Writer*, May–June 1877).

In time the use of French declined socially, and by Chekhov's day it was almost becoming a genteel vulgarism. It is typical that some of Chekhov's non-approved characters, including Natasha in *Three Sisters* (1900–1), should speak inaccurate French. The habit of using French names for Russian, for instance of addressing an Ivan as *Jean*, had also become a sign of social pretentiousness.

Improvidence and eccentricity

The gentry varied from impoverished squires, barely distinguishable in their way of life from their own few miserable serfs, to the Counts Sheremetev, largest serf-owners in the country. In the early nineteenth century Count D. N. Sheremetev owned nearly three hundred thousand serfs. His debts too were on the same gigantic scale, and he is said to have owed the sum of six million roubles in 1859 (Blum, pp. 370, 379).

To the Russian landowner grandiose debts seem to have been a symbol of superior status so that any mention of a country estate in nineteenth-century literature is likely to be followed by the information that it is heavily mortgaged and its owner hopelessly in debt. When emancipation took place, on the basis of redemption payments for land made by the peasants at rates favouring the landowners, this money was advanced to the owners by the government. Much of it was then swallowed up to meet their debts, and some was squandered on gigantic sprees in the watering-places of Europe.

These antics attracted the attention of Dostoyevsky, a frequent visitor to western Europe. According to him the Russian landowner with his vast retinue of maids and governesses, aroused the envy of observers from other countries, who did not realise that he was spending the last of his fortune on such ostentation.

These sybarites [Dostoyevsky wrote] who lounge around the German spas and the shores of Swiss lakes, these Luculli consuming their substance in Parisian restaurants – they themselves know, and even with some degree of pain foresee, that in the end they will run through their entire funds and that their children, these same little cherubs in English costumes, will perhaps have to beg alms throughout Europe, or turn into French or German labourers.

(Dostoyevsky, *Diary of a Writer*, May–June 1877).

Landowners' improvidence was encouraged by the government, which set up special banks to help the gentry and save it from the clutches of private money-lenders. Outrageously enough, there were even arrangements whereby charitable foundations loaned large sums to landowners out of funds subscribed for philanthropic purposes. Money lent to some landowners was pretty well a concealed gift. It was difficult, especially for a non-gentleman, to enforce payment of money owed by a member of the gentry, for many Russian gentlemen agreed with Count Vronsky in *Anna Karenin* that gambling debts were the only ones to be taken seriously by a man of honour. And the government was slow to foreclose on landowners' mortgages.

To improvidence must be added laziness and personal eccentricity as qualities of Russian landowners. Foreign observers were amazed at the hordes of servants with which Russian gentlemen surrounded themselves, and this in an age when gentlemen everywhere had a profusion of servants by modern standards. Waited on hand and foot, not needing even to fill their own tobacco-pipes, Russian landowners could easily become more like vegetables than men. Such, for example, is the life of the old couple portrayed in Gogol's *Old World Landowners* in his collection of stories *Mirgorod*. Such too is the sleepy atmosphere of the Russian countryside in *Oblomov's Dream*, the celebrated chapter from

Goncharov's novel depicting his lethargic hero's childhood on an estate where he is spoiled by relatives and servants in an over-protected atmosphere. The publication of *Oblomov* almost coincided with the end of serfdom, but life on the post-emancipation estate in Goncharov's later novel *The Precipice* is also a sleepy affair for much of the time.

So far as eccentricity is concerned, the grotesque landowners in Gogol's *Dead Souls* hold pride of place, but there is plenty of competition from other works providing variations on the same topic, such as Saltykov-Shchedrin's *Old Days in Poshekhonye* and *The Golovlyov Family*, portraying freakish landowners before and after emancipation. A real-life specimen in the early part of the nineteenth century was F. I. Tolstoy, nicknamed the American, of whom Herzen recounts that he once made his wife, a gypsy singer, stand on a table while he put a shot through the heel of her shoe to prove how good a marksman he was. He once seized a humble citizen with whom he was annoyed, bound him hand and foot and wrenched out one of his teeth. When the victim later dared to make an official complaint, Tolstoy bribed the police and the man found himself imprisoned for lodging false information. As Herzen so aptly comments: 'The stifling emptiness and dumbness of Russian life, curiously combined with its vitality and rumbustious character, give rise to all sorts of crackpot outbursts in our midst' (*My Past and Thoughts*, ch. xiv). So when Dostoyevsky's villain Stavrogin (in *Devils*) pulls a respectable middle-aged gentleman across the floor of the local club by his nose and is later found biting the ear of the provincial governor, his behaviour is to some extent traditional in an ex-officer and gentleman. So is that of Nozdryov in Gogol's *Dead Souls* when he orders his servants to beat Chichikov for refusing to finish a game of draughts in which he was being cheated. Such genteel pranks continued to enliven Russian life and fiction throughout the period studied here, for 'a Russian [as Dostoyevsky's narrator had commented in *Devils*] takes incredible delight in every kind of scandalous public upheaval.'

Treatment of serfs

Nineteenth-century landowners' powers over their serfs remained almost as uncontrolled as had been indicated by Catherine the Great in a letter to Diderot: 'Landowners do whatever seems good to them on their estates except inflict capital punishment; that is forbidden' (quoted in Sumner, p. 145). Even that provision was evaded because serfs were sometimes flogged to death.

A brief but vile episode relating to flogging and landowner-serf relations is recounted in Turgenev's *Manager*, one of his *Sportsman's Sketches*. A young squire and retired guards officer, Arkady Pavlovich Penochkin, finds himself served with red wine that turns out not to have been properly warmed by one of the servants, Fyodor. With no emotion and barely pausing from the polite conversation in which he is engaged, the master rings for another flunkey, a fat man with a low brow, and gives the instruction: 'About Fyodor . . . do the necessary' (i.e. flog him). He then turns back to his guest, remarking cheerily: '*Voilà, mon cher, les désagréments de la campagne*'. One unpleasant feature of this episode is that the punishment is ordered so casually and without, as it were, even the excuse of sadism.

The catalogue of outrages against serfs by landowners could be much extended. Siberian exile might be imposed by whim, as it was by Turgenev's mother on two of her serfs for failing to bow to her on some occasion. On a less savage level, Turgenev himself, a humane man whose *Sportsman's Sketches* may well have advanced the cause of emancipation, is reported to have bought a serf girl for seven hundred roubles for use as a concubine to help while away the tedium of exile to his country estate for writing his obituary of Gogol. More enterprising landowners kept harems of serf women. A market for serf girls, brought from various parts of Russia, existed in the industrial centre of Ivanovo for the benefit of textile tycoons, including industrialists who were themselves serfs (Blum, p. 427).

At the time of serfdom, landowners could prevent the marriage of serfs or make it conditional on paying a fee. They could marry a man and woman against their will – which might be thwarted if the couple heard of it in good time and could arrange to become godparents of the same child, thus debarred from marrying by ecclesiastical law. Some landowners threatened serfs with unwelcome marriages or conscription to extort money from them, having discreetly enquired into their means beforehand so as to know how much to charge. Though owners could connive at the acquisition of serfs by their own serfs, there was nothing to stop them simply taking such property back when they wished. Another unpleasant trick was to 'free' serfs grown too old for work, which just meant turning them out to fend for themselves. Thus serfs were sometimes treated worse than domestic animals.

Attempts were made under Alexander I and Nicholas I to limit landowners' power by regulations against arbitrary injustice. These measures included bans on splitting families by sale, on the public auction of serfs and on the sale of peasants without land, but they were widely evaded. The trouble was that serfs had no effective means of appeal against landowners, even to enforce their meagre rights in law. Hence the many outbreaks of peasant violence – about eight hundred in the years 1845 to 1860 – and the numerous murders of landowners, including Dostoyevsky's father, and their managers by serfs.

Many members of the gentry were absentee landlords who, in extreme cases, might never have visited some of their estates, or who confined themselves like Oblomov to communicating with their bailiffs. But there were some landowners eager to improve their properties and bring in modern methods. Journals and societies were formed to promote agriculture. Even though all this left most squires untouched, the 'good' landowner does figure in fiction, trying to bridge the great gap in communication between squire and peasant. In particular Tolstoy's first-hand experience of the problem on his own land provided material for much of his writing from his early story *Morning of a Landowner* (1856) onwards, and two examples of his 'good' landowners are mentioned above (p. 129). That a landowner in the late nineteenth century need not necessarily qualify by his fecklessness to be a typical owner of a cherry orchard is shown by Alyokhin, the hard-working squire in Chekhov's story *About Love* (1898).

Besides monsters of idleness, profligacy, cruelty and eccentricity, the Russian gentry also produced many humane and sensitive men, including the very writers who portray the gentry's own faults with such skill. As the most articulate class, the gentry dominated cultural and intellectual life, even providing its own would-be gravediggers. It was not necessary to scratch an anarchist such as Peter Kropotkin or a regicide like Sophia Perovsky, one of Alexander II's assassins, to find a prince's son and a provincial governor's daughter. Thus various levels of activity are involved among scions of the Russian gentry, from the near-paralysis of the fictional Oblomov to the active real-life Bakunin, escapee from Siberia, stoker of the fires of European revolution and rival of Karl Marx within the First Socialist International.

11 Religion

Church and state

The Empire had an established church, the Russian Orthodox Church, of which the Tsar was the official defender, and in a sense the head. But his position was not comparable to that of the Pope in the Roman Catholic Church. The Tsar's function was to protect dogma, and he was not empowered to change it, and though he attended divine service, he could not officiate.

Just as the state became increasingly multi-national through territorial expansion, so expansion also rendered it increasingly multi-religious. The accession of the Baltic lands had brought in many additional Protestants, and the annexations of Poland introduced Catholic and Jewish citizens, of whom there had been hardly any previously. Then the conquest of Central Asia enlarged the Mohammedan component. But the Orthodox Church remained predominant, as shown by the following breakdown of the population of the Empire according to the main religious persuasions in percentages relating to the beginning of the twentieth century (from Kovalevsky, p. 66):

Orthodox	71 per cent
Catholic	9 per cent
Protestant	5 per cent
Jews	3 per cent
Mohammedan	9 per cent

The proportion of over seventy per cent of Orthodox Christians requires comment. It includes many persons explicitly opposed to the official Orthodox faith (the so-called Old Believers) and also sectarians who had no links with Orthodoxy at all. The numbers of Old Believers and sectarians are hard to establish because of the inducements to play down their importance in official estimates. Some have even put the figure as high as twenty or twenty-five million at the beginning of the twentieth century, although the official number was recorded in the 1897 census as being only a little over two million (Kolarz, pp. 128–9). Still, the Russian

Orthodox Church remained dominant numerically, as well as representing the official state religion.

It had held this position since 988 A D, when Vladimir, Grand Prince of Kiev, made Christianity the official religion of Old Russia. When the Greek and Roman churches divided in 1054, the Russians sided with the former, a decision of much consequence to their cultural history which thereafter developed along different lines from that of western Europe. But the Russian Church did not remain a subordinate branch of the Greek, and when Constantinople was captured by the Turks in 1453 Russia became ecclesiastically independent in practice. This independence was formalised in 1589 when the office of Patriarch of Moscow was created. In 1721 the patriarchate was abolished by Peter the Great, who set up in its place a body called the Most Holy Governing Synod – until 1917 the governing body of the Russian Orthodox Church. The secularisation of church lands had been completed in 1764.

Of the church's submissiveness to the state in the nineteenth century many instances can be quoted. During the Decembrist revolt, while insurgent troops were defying the Tsar in St Petersburg, 'many of the clergy of the capital, with the metropolitan at their head, went in full vestments, cross in hand, to urge the rebels to submit' (Curtiss, p. 30). The Metropolitan Filaret of Moscow, a notoriously reactionary prelate, opposed the abolition of flogging – and of serfdom too until the last moment, when he changed his mind just in time and helped to draw up the emancipation manifesto of 1861. After Turgenev's death in 1883, young priests were required by the Synod and bishops to curb their enthusiasm, as expressed in obituary sermons, for this representative of Russian liberalism. This last episode does at least show that not all elements in the Orthodox Church were entirely subservient to the state.

The Orthodox Church in literature

Of the better-known nineteenth-century authors, Leskov covers the richness and variety of Russian religion especially well in many ories and sketches, his descriptions of religious life being by no eans confined to that of the official church. He has given a rticularly detailed picture of a priest's tribulations in the novel *athedral Folk*. Another sympathetic portrait of a church dignitary is to be found in *The Bishop* (1902) by Chekhov, who seems o have been an agnostic, but was not anti-clerical and accepted e Orthodox Church as a part of Russian life. Tolstoy was less -operatively disposed. He left a scathing satire of Orthodox hurch ritual in *Resurrection*, and his non-fictional religious orks, such as *Confession*, first published in Geneva in 1884, *A riticism of Dogmatic Theology* and *What I Believe*, could not be rought out in Russia at the time when they were written. It will lso be remembered that Tolstoy enjoyed the distinction of being xcommunicated in 1901. His clash with the church derives from is advocacy of rational Christianity based on Gospel teaching, ut free from later accretions. The Orthodox Church with its pectacular ritual was far removed from his idea of religion.

Organisation

he Synod, the governing body of the Church, consisted of cclesiastical dignitaries, but did not have a fixed number of nembers. The Metropolitan of St Petersburg was usually its hairman and the Metropolitans of Moscow and Kiev were also nembers, as was the Exarch of Georgia. Other members included rchbishops, bishops or abbots appointed by the Tsar and two enior members of the white clergy (see p. 147), of which one was sually the Tsar's confessor. But the key figure, also appointed by he Tsar, was a layman – the so-called chief procurator, whose pproval was required for all the Synod's decisions and who ecame in practice a sort of minister of religion – and indeed njoyed the official status of minister. The most famous chief rocurator (1880–1905) was Konstantin Pobedonostsev who, as lready mentioned, became one of the most powerful figures in Russia after the Tsar. The Synod controlled higher church appoint-

ments, ecclesiastical schools and ecclesiastical censorship. I
ensured that the Church remained a docile instrument of the state
throughout the nineteenth century.

There were about sixty dioceses in all, of which three – those of
St Petersburg, Moscow and Kiev – came under metropolitans,
while nineteen were archbishoprics and the rest bishoprics.
Within each diocese a consistory and chancery, with a lay secretary
responsible to the chief procurator, ensured that policy percolated
down to individual parishes. The consistory administered church
schools and seminaries within the diocese and was responsible for
the ecclesiastical courts in which divorce cases were heard.

The Orthodox clergy

The clergy, together with the gentry, formed one of the two estates
officially privileged by exemption from personal taxation, recruitment into the army and corporal punishment (see p. 110). For
various reasons the enjoyment of these concessions might be
limited so far as the clergy was concerned, and in any case no one

Far left. Nicholas Dobrolyubov (right) and his father. Like many leading radicals, Dobrolyubov was the son of a parish priest. His father was a member of the white clergy for whom marriage was compulsory. Dobrolyubov senior wears the priest's tall hat called the *kamilavka.*
Left. The Metropolitan of Moscow, 1856. High offices of the Orthodox Church were the preserve of the so-called black clergy, who were celibate.

familiar with western European conditions would have thought of Russian parish priests as privileged persons.

The clergy fell into two classes, popularly termed white and black. The black clergy were monks dedicated to celibacy, while for white clergy marriage was not only permitted, but was compulsory before they could be ordained. A priest must marry a spinster and was not permitted a second marriage – if his wife died he must become a monk or church servitor, or else leave the church. Though the black clergy did wear black clothes, it would be wrong to infer that members of the white clergy were therefore clad in white, for they too wore black or at least sub-fusc. Both had full beards and kept their hair long. What chiefly distinguished them, besides marital status, was that members of the black clergy might aspire to high office as abbot, archimandrite, bishop, archbishop or metropolitan, whereas a white cleric must remain a humble parish priest denied promotion beyond the rank of senior priest, or of superintendent priest with supervisory duties over several parishes.

As the following figures show, the nineteenth century saw a

decline in the numbers of the clergy in relation to the population as a whole. The numbers of the white clergy also declined absolutely, while an increase in the actual numbers of the black did not keep pace with the growth of the population (from Milyukov, i, p. 147).

| | *Actual figures* | | *As per 100,000 inhabitants of Orthodox faith* | |
	1840	*1890*	*1840*	*1890*
White clergy	116,728	96,892	265	137
Monks, nuns and novices	15,251	40,286	56	34

The clergy almost formed a caste within Russian society. Any white priest was likely to be a priest's son and to be married to a priest's daughter, while their children were educated separately from the population at large in special teaching establishments. Though not closed to children from other estates, these were free to the clergy – church schools (*dukhovnyye uchilishcha*) for younger boys, and then seminaries for older, the latter being a sort of combined upper school and college. There were also special diocesan schools for daughters of the clergy. Would-be white seminarists sought to marry priests' daughters who, with luck, might bring the parish of a defunct or retired father as a dowry, assuming that the bishop and his consistory (who tended to acquire the function of unofficial marriage brokers) were agreed. The black clergy too was recruited from the seminaries, where young men were faced with a choice: either an ambitious church career or married bliss, but not both.

Provisions made under Alexander II to throw the church open to entrants from outside the clergy did not lead to a rush of applicants, and seminarists continued to provide most new recruits. But though nearly all priests were ex-seminarists, it by no means follows that all seminarists became priests. Many joined the anti-clerical intelligentsia, and some figured in literature – it will be remembered that two of Russia's best-known radical thinkers and literary critics, Dobrolyubov and Chernyshevsky, were sons of priests. Most famous of all seminarists and one acclaimed by some as a universal genius, was the product of a nineteenth-century Georgian seminary who happened not to be a priest's son – Joseph Stalin, then known as Dzhugashvili. As this instance shows, church schools and seminaries were not always successful in instilling conventional piety. They were often indecorous institutions where drunkenness, violence and cruelty were common. One well-known description of life at a church school in the mid-century gives a lurid picture of its sordid possibilities: *Sketches of a Church School* (1862–3) by N. G. Pomyalovsky. An ex-seminarist, he drank himself to death when he was twenty-eight and his book reflects memories of school-days more unseemly than Tom Brown's.

The seminaries kept to the nineteenth-century Russian student tradition of unruliness. In 1885 the Metropolitan of Moscow had to call in the police to quell rioting seminarists, who were severely beaten in his presence with rods which, according to rumour, he had personally consecrated for the purpose. A few years later the seminarists of Voronezh tried to blow up their rector with a bomb placed in a stove (Leroy-Beaulieu, pp. 269–70). Thus the Russian seminary moved with the times, and it is not surprising if it was sometimes thought of as a nursery of revolution.

Once established in a parish, the priest found his surroundings little more edifying than they had been in his college days. He might occupy the humble hut which had belonged to his predecessor, now perhaps his father-in-law. He might also be allotted a few acres of land which he could till like his parishioners, or rent out if he wished. But he had no staple income. The state did dispense meagre funds for the upkeep of parish priests, but many received nothing, for such subsidies were generally channelled to parishes where competition from some rival persuasion had to be taken into account. Hence the practice whereby the priest made charges for christening, marrying, burying and so on. There was no fixed tariff, and so it was usual to haggle over the price. Thus there were stories of young people turning up at church to be

married, but coming away still unwed because they could not strike a bargain with the priest. Underpaid for a blessing, priests might substitute a curse unless they got more money.

On major holidays such as Christmas and Easter the priest would tour his parish resplendent in chasuble and stole, and accompanied by various minions. Entering each hut in turn, he would face the icon, intone a prayer or two, pocket what was in effect a tip, and move on. It was of such processions that Chekhov wrote in *Peasants*: 'Those who had not fasted and prepared for communion in Lent were charged fifteen copecks apiece by the parish priest when he went round the huts with the cross at Easter.'

Sometimes the priest's steps might become less firm as these processions continued. Russian peasants had crude notions of hospitality, and to refuse a glass or two of vodka was to insult them. This was in any case not an insult which many priests were inclined by temperament to offer, so that they often staggered round their parishes hopelessly drunk. Next day the very peasant who had been most insistent in plying his priest with liquor would be the first to make fun of him because he could not hold his drink. Herzen has a story of a parish priest so addicted to hard liquor that, after officiating at a wedding or christening in an outlying village, he was often carried off unconscious by the peasants, and dumped in his cart like a sheaf of corn to be taken home by his horse, which was used to all this and knew the way back without needing a driver (*My Past and Thoughts*, ch. xxviii).

As this shows, the average priest enjoyed little respect from his fellows, though his status in the towns might be less lowly than in the country. The Russian landowner looked down on the priest as an inferior, and was quite capable of having him ducked in the village pond to provide amusement for his guests. Peasants thought it unlucky to meet a priest in the street and coined sayings to illustrate the greed of the *pop* (the disrespectful word by which the parish priest, more politely termed *svyashchennik*, was known). But there were other even lowlier figures among the clergy. There was the deacon or priest's assistant, who helped to perform services, could himself carry out certain functions such as conducting funerals, and was expected to have a rich bass voice. Yet humbler were the church servitors, consisting of sextons, bell-ringers, psalm singers and readers. Persons of all these categories had the right to send their children to the free church schools and seminaries.

Though village priests and their minions were often regarded with genial contempt, it is important to note that Russian peasants did not transfer to religion itself the feelings with which they regarded its representatives.

Appearance and decoration of churches

Orthodox churches were rectangular in plan, or cruciform, and might have a number of onion-domes, gilded or painted in a bright colour, usually blue or green, and surmounted by a Greek cross. There might be a bell-tower. The chancel or sanctuary, that

Below. Wooden churches at Belaya Slyuda, Archangel Province. With their characteristic bizarre onion-dome outline, Russian churches help to diversify the horizon of the flat Russian plain. *Right*. Interior of a wooden church.

The iconostasis is the screen beyond the kneeling figures, with the 'Tsar's Gate' in the middle. The congregation stands during an Orthodox service and the singing is done by clergy and choir. The liturgy is in a special language, Church Slavonic, but sermons (which occupy a minor role) are given in Russian.

is the eastern part of the church for the use of the officiating priest and his assistants, is confusingly termed *altar* in Russian. The altar itself is called a throne (*prestol*). The chancel is separated from the body of the church by a screen on which icons are hung, called the iconostasis and containing three doors, of which the central one is the 'Tsar's gate', through which only the priest may pass. In front of this on the congregation's side is a raised platform, the ambo, from which prayers, readings and sermons are delivered. If there was a special choir to supplement the singing done by priests and servitors, it would normally be housed in a balcony at the back (west end) of the church.

A large part was played in the Orthodox Church by the cult of icons, consisting of half-length pictures of Jesus Christ, the Madonna or a saint, executed in a stylised manner deriving originally from Byzantine tradition. They varied in size from about a square inch to several square feet, and the part of the picture representing clothes might be covered with an embossed metal plaque. Icons could be humble, such as those turned out in tens of thousands by the cottage industry of Vladimir province, and as mentioned above, peasant huts were incomplete without their icons. More valuable icons, often richly ornamented, were found in churches, including miracle-working icons, object of their own special cult. Some, including the icon of the Kazan Madonna, had feast days in their honour. And some, like the Smolensk Madonna, taken round with the Russian army during the war against Napoleon in 1812, were associated with martial glory and could be credited with such triumphs as the French retreat from Moscow. Previously the Vladimir Madonna had reputedly saved Moscow from the Tatars. Icons were sometimes paraded round the fields to discourage drought. During the anti-Jewish pogroms at the end of the nineteenth century it was prudent to have an icon handy, because by waving it out of the window one could show the yelling mob that one was a fellow-Christian and thus hope to save family and shop from insult, injury, looting or death.

Icons were displayed in churches and commonly had a lamp burning in front of them. Candles too were prominent in the church, both decoratively and financially. It was usual for the congregation to buy candles, often manufactured by the church and a source of revenue. The glitter of lamps and candles, the austere beauty of the icons, the magnificent vestments of priests and acolytes, the superb singing and the solemn atmosphere of the service – all combined to lend majesty to Orthodox Church services. In a small village things could not be as lavishly managed as in one of the chief monasteries or metropolitan cathedrals, but the service was impressive enough to give the ill-used Russian peasant a glimpse of something quite unlike his daily life.

Services, ritual and sacraments

When officiating at services the clergy and their assistants wore a surplice, the *stikhar*. On top of this the priest wore a chasuble or sleeveless robe, while deacons wore a stole over one shoulder. A different kind of stole was worn by the priest under his chasuble and fell over both shoulders. As headgear the priest wore a soft hat, of black or purple velvet, coming to a point on top, called *skufya*, or else a tall hat called a *kamilavka*. A bishop wore a mitre and a long cope and carried a crozier.

In the Orthodox service the congregation stood, and there were no pews, organ or statuary. Otherwise austerity was at a discount. Singing by clergy and choir, unaccompanied by instruments or congregation and often magnificently impressive, occupied a prominent part in the service, while sermons by the priest were of little account, though not unknown. A linguistically sophisticated visitor would also detect that, though any sermon would be delivered in Russian, the liturgy was couched in a different but related tongue, Church Slavonic. The visitor would also notice that the liturgy occupied a great deal of time, so that church services, especially vespers, were lengthy affairs.

Confession was soon over, but was by no means considered a mere formality, even though special confessional boxes were not used. Parishioners often queued up to confess, and each would answer one or two questions, after which he would receive absolution with the laying on of a corner of the priest's stole on his head. Then he would kiss the cross and the Gospel, and give his name to the deacon, who kept a list. At communion the members of the congregation, as well as the priest, partook of bread and wine. The bread, in the form of specially baked small loaves (*prosfory*), was broken in pieces and placed in the wine, intinction being the technical name for this procedure. The priest would ladle a spoonful of wine, containing a piece of the soaked bread, into the mouth of each communicant, and communicants would also take a piece of the bread and consume it as they turned away. A peasant described in Dostoyevsky's *Diary of a Writer* (1873, ch. v) was induced, for a 'dare', to smuggle his piece of wine-soaked bread out of church and aim a shot-gun at it after it had been placed on a stick stuck in the ground – perhaps the most weird among Dostoyevsky's many descriptions of sacrilegious acts.

The Orthodox wedding ceremony was elaborate. Bride and bridegroom wore crowns, exchanged rings, drank three times alternately from the same cup and were paraded three times round the church, their hands clasped for them by the priest. A well-known fictional description of an Orthodox wedding – that of Levin and Kitty Oblonsky – occurs in Tolstoy's *Anna Karenin*. Christening was combined with confirmation, and triple total immersion was the practice. At funeral services the dead were exposed to view in open coffins. It was this procedure which made it possible for Hermann, hero of Pushkin's *Queen of Spades* (1834), to receive the impression that his victim, the deceased countess, winked at him when he bowed his farewell to her on the occasion of her funeral.

It will be remembered (see p. 124) that church festivals were numerous, the most important being Easter, with which many traditional practices, culinary, liturgical and osculatory, were associated. The Easter kiss exchanged between members of the congregation at the end of the service on Easter eve, and the prescribed dialogue ('Christ has arisen'; 'In truth he has arisen') form an episode in the seduction of Catherine Maslov in Tolstoy's *Resurrection*.

Monks

Though only monks could rise to high ecclesiastical office, the average Russian monk was a humble individual who lacked such ambition or opportunity. Considering the importance of monasteries in earlier Russian history, monks and nuns, numbering in 1890 only about forty thousand of both sexes (with a preponderance of nuns) were remarkably few in number and simple in organisation. They had only one monastic rule and many monasteries and convents were small. But three were large and outstanding, being called *lavry* and associated with a past or present capital of Russia. These were the Monastery of the Caves at Kiev, the Monastery of the Trinity and St Sergius near Moscow, and the Monastery of St Alexander Nevsky at St Petersburg. Other famous monasteries included a fourth *lavra*, that of Pochayev in the western Ukraine, the Solovetsky Monastery on islands in the White Sea, and that of Optina Pustyn in central Russia. The last-named was noted for an institution which interested Dostoyevsky: that of tutorship by older monks termed elders (*startsy*) over younger. The best-known monastery in Russian fiction is that in *The Brothers Karamazov*. Here Dostoyevsky portrays a young novice, Alyosha Karamazov, and the influence exercised over him by the *starets* Father Zosima, who had been an army officer before entering the monastery. Another well-known fictional recruit to the life of religious hermit was also a former army officer – Tolstoy's Father Sergius in his posthumous story of the same name.

Old Believers

The Old Believers, sometimes called Old Ritualists or Schismatics, were an important social and religious phenomenon. They originated with the schism which occurred in the Russian Orthodox Church in 1667, when approval was given to the revision of Russian church books undertaken at the instigation of the Patriarch Nikon by collation with the Greek originals from which they were derived, but had since greatly diverged. Old Believers were those who rejected the newly corrected versions and clung to various practices which came to distinguish them from the Orthodox. Old Belief rallied Russian conservatism and distrust of foreigners, whether Greek or not, among the less educated, but the issues dividing Orthodoxy and Old Belief now seem utterly trivial. Thus the Old Believers crossed themselves with two fingers and sang Hallelujah twice, while the Orthodox crossed themselves with three fingers and sang Hallelujah thrice. There were differences in pronouncing the name Jesus, in the depiction of the Cross and so on. In the early days Old Believers might go to the stake or have their tongues ripped out rather than cross themselves with the wrong number of fingers, and though such punishment was not meted out in the nineteenth century, they continued to suffer severe discrimination and persecution while clinging to their own version of the liturgy and ritual.

Old Believers were conservative in other ways besides ritual, having defied Peter the Great by keeping their beards and old-fashioned caftans. They were mainly of Great Russian origin and consisted of peasants, merchants and Cossacks, hardly ever of gentry. They eschewed tobacco and also, though not total abstainers, drinking orgies. Many succeeded in business and built palatial residences in Moscow, and their sobriety and business acumen have caused them to be compared with British Quakers and Methodists. They have been claimed as quintessentially Russian and their main centres were in the suburbs of Moscow, regarded as a more Russian city than St Petersburg. Outside the Moscow area there were numerous Old Believers in the north of European Russia, on the Volga, and also among the miners of the Urals, the Cossacks of the south-east of European Russia and the colonisers of Siberia.

The Old Believers were a mixed group, falling into two main classes depending on whether they made use of priests or not. It happened that there were no Old Believer bishops for two centuries after the outbreak of the schism, which made it impossible to ordain Old Believer priests. So the priestists relied on 'runaway' Orthodox priests to perform marriage services and other sacraments. In the 1860s they secured the services of a co-operative Orthodox prelate, Metropolitan Ambrose of the Church of Bosnia, who consecrated three Old Believers as bishops at Bela Krinica, then on Austrian territory. The ordination of Old Believer priests thus became possible and ensured for the future, but not all priestists would accept Bela Krinica and a minority of 'runaway-

An Old Believer. The Old Believers originated in the seventeenth century as the result of a decision to revise church books. They were in origin mainly Great Russian peasants, Cossacks or merchants, and were traditionally Russian in their ways, as opposed to the europeanised gentry.

priestists' continued as before. The priestless were a less organised group. They had no sacraments or marriage, tended to believe that the reign of Antichrist had come about on earth, expected the imminent end of the world, avoided persons of other religious persuasions, and – in extreme cases in the early days – shut themselves in churches or huts and burnt themselves alive.

Leskov's *Sealed Angel* (1873), telling of the adventures of an icon confiscated by the police and restored to the faithful by a miracle, is a well-known story dealing with Old Believers, but the greatest fictional chronicler of Old Belief is P. I. Melnikov-Pechersky, whose long novels *In the Forests* (1871–5) and *In the Hills* (1875–81) describe their communities on the Volga.

Other denominations and sectarians

The religious sects, of which a great variety existed, were distinct from the Old Believers. The most numerous group was that of the Molokans, so called because it was their practice to drink milk (*moloko*) during fasts, in contrast with Orthodox Christians. The sect had over a million members at the beginning of the twentieth century. This was a sober and fairly prosperous community, living mainly in the Caucasus and basing its teaching on the Bible and the practice of the early apostolic church. Members of another sect, that of the Dukhobors, managed to emigrate to Canada through the generosity of Tolstoy in making over to them profits from *Resurrection*. They thus became the one Russian sect better known abroad than in Russia itself, largely for their disobedience to civil authority and habit of removing their clothes in public. Other sects included the Flagellants or Khlysty, their name probably being a popular corruption of *Khristy* (Christs), which was how the men referred to each other. They were in any case less given to flagellation than to dancing provocative of religious ecstasy. They danced with a rotary motion, whereas others, the jumpers (*skakuny*), bobbed up and down. In the more enthusiastic gatherings such episodes might end in sexual orgies, as shown in one of Chekhov's stories, *Murder* (1895). At the other extreme was the sect of Eunuchs (*skoptsy*) who practised castration, a proceeding which did at least keep their numbers under control.

In the 1860s a Russian evangelical movement arose in the Ukraine, the Caucasus and St Petersburg. In the Ukraine this started as a movement called Shtundism under the influence of German colonists in the area and of their Lutheran and Mennonite pastors. In St Petersburg evangelicism made headway in aristocratic circles, influenced by an Englishman, Lord Radstock, and an anglicised German, Dr Friedrich Baedeker. Dostoyevsky wrote about Radstock in his *Diary of a Writer* for March 1876, and an evangelist portrayed in *Resurrection* was suggested to Tolstoy by Baedeker. The Union of Russian Baptists was founded in 1884 in

The Icon of the Korsun Madonna, painted about 1700. Icons were commonly displayed in Russian Orthodox churches, in the humblest dwellings and even in the *traktir* or Russian pub'. When entering a peasant hut it was normal good manners to face the icon in the 'red' (or 'front') corner and cross oneself.

the Ukraine, but remained illegal until 1905, when a period of greater religious tolerance began.

As this reminds one, nineteenth-century Russia enjoyed little denominational freedom. Natural as it might seem for non-Russian citizens to follow some outlandish creed, a Russian was expected to be Orthodox. So missionary work by the Orthodox Church was encouraged, while proselytising by non-Orthodox persuasions was forbidden by law. But the tolerance extended to non-Russians in religious matters meant, for example, that Roman Catholics on Russian soil could usually find a place of worship. 'Throughout European Russia . . . there was hardly a large town without its Catholic church or chapel' (Kolarz, p. 180). Catholic churches were to be found in Siberia and Central Asia too – in Tashkent, Tomsk, Tobolsk, Irkutsk and Vladivostok. These were not built for Russians, but for Catholic Poles, Lithuanians and other non-Russians. Still, tolerance had its limits. Non-Russians, especially in Poland itself, were subject to state interference with the practice of non-Orthodox religions, and this severity became especially marked towards the end of the nineteenth century.

One result of the docility of the Orthodox Church in fulfilling demands made by the government, was that politically disaffected intellectuals tended to be anti-clerical, church and state being lumped together in their minds as equally pernicious.

12 Towns

Growth of urban population

Though most Russians were countrymen, the population of the towns was growing fast in the eighteenth and nineteenth centuries – more than six times as rapidly as that of the countryside. The following figures show the increase of Russian urban population and the way in which it was rising as a percentage of the whole (from Kovalevsky, p. 60):

Year	Number of town-dwellers	Percentage of whole population
1812	1,653,000	4·4
1835	3,025,000	5·8
1851	3,482,000	7·8
1867	8,157,000	10·6
1897	16,785,212	13·0

There were few large towns. In 1867 there were only four in the whole Empire with a population of over one hundred thousand (St Petersburg, Moscow, Warsaw and Odessa), and even then one of those was Polish. By 1897 the number (of towns in the Empire with a population over one hundred thousand) had risen to nineteen. These were, in descending order of size: St Petersburg, Moscow, Warsaw, Odessa, Lodz, Riga, Kiev, Kharkov, Tiflis, Vilna, Tashkent, Saratov, Kazan, Yekaterinoslav (now Dnepropetrovsk), Rostov-on-Don, Astrakhan, Baku, Tula and Kishinyov. By no means all the above towns were fully or even partly Russian, though all belonged to the Empire.

Appearance and general atmosphere

Observers from western Europe hardly recognised Russian towns as towns at all. Less tactful foreigners, and some Russians too, described Moscow itself or even the whole Empire as one vast village. Observers also noted a lack of variety in Russian towns.

High life in Moscow.
A gala performance at the
theatre. Part of the celebrations
for Alexander II's coronation.

Ample available space and danger of fire encouraged a tendency to sprawl, and the wide unpaved streets were often no better than those found in ordinary villages. Paved roads, sewage systems, street lighting and piped water were not unheard of, but even by the beginning of the twentieth century they were still restricted to small, prosperous sections of the larger towns.

Most houses were single-storied and made of wood, but stone-built apartment houses of several storeys were also going up in the towns where population pressure was greatest. It was common practice to rent apartments and houses rather than to own them, and the more salubrious might be occupied by wealthy officials, while the very poorest citizens might have to hire the corner of a room in some unsavoury doss-house. Among these that of Khitrov Market in Moscow was a notorious haunt of tramps, prostitutes and thieves. Here professional beggar-women could hire emaciated babies by the day to attract alms from passers-by, and if the baby died during the course of the day they would continue exhibiting it so as to get their money's worth (Troyat, p. 61).

Despite such grotesque examples of private enterprise, the general atmosphere of Russian towns was torpid. There were few shops as understood in western Europe, shopping often being done in markets consisting of small, ill-lit stores, each exactly like its neighbour and known as the trading rows. As in some villages, churches with painted domes and characteristic outlines might supply variety to the eye. And in provincial capitals the governor's residence, court of justice, administrative offices, gymnasiums (grammar schools), hospitals, theatres and so on provided a relatively imposing centre to the sprawling, ramshackle outskirts.

The two capitals

Two giants stood out among Russian towns and cities: the capital, St Petersburg, and the old capital, Moscow. Both were well over the million mark in population in 1897, when St Petersburg had 1,267,023 inhabitants and Moscow 1,035,664 – compare London,

A view of Moscow in the 1880s.
The old Russian capital, with its Kremlin
and 'forty times forty' churches, was also
the headquarters of the Slavophiles and
Old Believers. Muscovites thought of themselves
as being more Russian than St Petersburgers.

New York and Paris at the turn of the century, with 6,581,000, 3,437,000 and 2,660,000 respectively. The nearest rival to St Petersburg and Moscow among Russian cities was Odessa with a mere 405,041 souls, less than a third as big as St Petersburg. The Tsars continued to be crowned in Moscow, and the habit of referring even in official documents to St Petersburg and Moscow as the two capitals, showed that Russians had not forgotten where the government seat had been before Peter the Great moved it in 1712.

The contrast between the two chief cities has been pointed out again and again. St Petersburg, Russia's 'window on Europe', was the more cosmopolitan, slick, fashionable and up-to-date. Its population included many government officials and foreigners, while its status as a port and seat of the Russian court helped to make it magnificent and exotic. If St Petersburgers called Moscow the largest village in the Empire, Muscovites could retort by claiming themselves more truly Russian. With its historical Kremlin and many churches or cathedrals ('forty times forty' according to legend), Moscow had a special hold on Russian affections. It was often called 'Mother' Moscow, an epithet that no one would think of applying to the frigid and stately St Petersburg, which in any case belongs to the wrong grammatical gender. St Petersburg too did have its affectionate nickname, *Piter*, deriving from the Dutch form of Peter the Great's name. Moscow was the headquarters of groups disapproving of Peter's reforming and europeanising activities – the slavophiles and the Old Believers. These were often thought to be the most Russian Russians. Herzen said that Petersburgers used to laugh at Muscovites' clothes, at their long hair and the shape of their whiskers. 'Moscow [he wrote] is a civilian city, rather dissolute, unused to discipline.' St Petersburg on the other hand was like an army barracks. Everyone dressed identically. 'If you were to show an Englishman these battalions of tightly-buttoned slickers in identical frock-coats on the Nevsky Prospekt [the city's most celebrated thoroughfare], he would think they were a squad of policemen' (*My Past and Thoughts*, ch. xxvi).

By the end of the century both capitals were centres of thriving
industries. Moscow formed the core of the Central Industrial
Region, devoted mainly to light industry and including the towns
or industrial settlements of Tula, Yaroslavl, Orekhovo-Zuyevo,
and Ivanovo-Voznesensk, 'the Russian Manchester'. St Petersburg
was an important centre of the machine-tool industry. But it is not
these aspects of the two capitals which are most richly illustrated
by the best-known Russian classical authors.

The greatest invocation of the imperial capital, that in Pushkin's
Bronze Horseman (written in 1833), is solemn and rhetorical,
paying only passing attention to the capital's economic poten-
tialities. The same author's *Eugene Onegin* begins and ends with
the social whirl of St Petersburg, but also includes vivid pictures
of the Russian countryside and of Muscovite society. Though
Gogol began his career by describing the Ukrainian countryside,
some of his most notable work is found in his St Petersburg
stories, of which the best-known are *The Nose* and *Nevsky Prospekt*
(both 1835) and above all *The Overcoat* (1842). Dostoyevsky was

brought up in Moscow, but became an enthusiastic St Petersburger, making the city a background for much of his early work describing the woes of petty officials and young men who rent miserable little rooms or corners of rooms in the slums. An impressive picture of the city from his mature period is that in *Crime and Punishment*, set near the unsavoury Haymarket (*Sennaya ploshchad*).

Tolstoy differed from Dostoyevsky in finding country air sweeter than that of St Petersburg's tenements, but the two capitals figure as the background for much of *War and Peace* and *Anna Karenin*. It is fashionable city life that Tolstoy describes in his great novels – the world of counts, princes, hostesses, high officials and guards officers. Of the squalid side of city life he was, by his own confession, ignorant when he wrote *War and Peace* and *Anna Karenin*, for in his later *What then must we do?* (completed in 1886) he states: 'I had spent my life in the country and when I came to live in Moscow in 1881 the sight of urban poverty surprised me.' In this work Tolstoy describes the impression made by Moscow doss-houses, the Lyapin and Rzhanov Houses, which he visited after volunteering to help collect statistics for the census of 1882.

Left. A view of St Nicholas's Church in St Petersburg, 1839, showing the Fontanka Canal. Even in the capital city paved streets were an exception. Water transport was an important part of the Empire's economy and timber (as in the picture) for fuel and building, was an important freight. *Below*. High life in the 1850s. A ball in the Gentry's Assembly Rooms.

Provincial towns

Russian novelists were cautious about identifying provincial towns, preferring to call them 'the town of N.' (or any other letter of the alphabet). Or such places may, like the setting of Dostoyevsky's *Devils* and the town in Chekhov's *My Life*, be called simply 'our town'. The identity of the town which forms the centre of Chichikov's intrigues in *Dead Souls* is concealed, but it was conceivably suggested to the author by Kursk. Similarly the identity of the provincial capital in *Three Sisters* is not revealed in the text of the play, though Chekhov did tell Gorky that 'the action takes place in a provincial town such as Perm' (letter of 16th October 1900). The trouble is that there were so many Kursks and Perms in Russia with little to differentiate one from another. 'In Russia all towns are identical [Chekhov once wrote to his sister from Yekaterinburg – now Sverdlovsk]. Yekaterinburg is just like Perm or Tula. It's also like Sumy and Galyach' (letter of 29th April 1890). Even his

home town Taganrog impressed Chekhov as boring, though it was a port on the sea of Azov with a polyglot population of sailors and merchants, including Greeks, Armenians and Bulgarians. It had quite a good theatre too and a passable library, but to Chekhov it was completely Asiatic, a place where people 'do nothing but eat, sleep and multiply and have no other interests' (letter of 7th April 1887). Chekhov's works abound in denunciations of provincial Russian towns so outspoken that it is no wonder if he was cryptic about their identity. One such speech is that delivered by Andrew Prozorov in Act Four of *Three Sisters*. 'All these people do,' he says, repeating a familiar Chekhovian motif, 'is eat, drink and sleep till they drop down dead.' Another such Chekhovian diatribe is that found in *My Life*:

What kept these sixty-five thousand people going? That's what I couldn't see. Kimry got its living by boots, I knew. Tula made samovars and guns, Odessa was a port. But what our town was and what it did, I had no idea. Great Dvoryansky Street and a couple of the smarter streets were kept going on capital and civil servants' salaries paid by the government. But what of the other eight streets that ran parallel for a couple of miles and vanished behind the hill? What did they live on? That's what baffled me.

The way these people lived was shameful beyond words. There was no park, no theatre, no decent orchestra. No one went inside the town library or club reading-room except for a few Jewish youths, so magazines and new books lay around uncut for months. Well-off professional people slept in cramped, stuffy bedrooms on wooden, bug-infested beds. They kept their children in revoltingly dirty rooms called nurseries, and servants, even old and respected ones, slept on the kitchen floor under rags. On fast-days their houses smelled of sturgeon fried in sunflower oil and on other days of borshch. Their food tasted awful and their drinking-water was unwholesome. At the town hall, governor's office, bishop's palace and all over town they had been going on for years about how we had no good, cheap water and must borrow two hundred thousand roubles from the government to lay on a proper supply. Very rich people – our town had about three dozen, who were known to gamble away whole estates at cards – also drank tainted water and talked excitedly about this loan, in fact they never stopped. It made no sense to me. I

Playbill for a performance of Gogol's *Inspector-General* at Taganrog Theatre in 1871. Chekhov attended this performance as a boy of eleven.

should have thought they would have found it easier to go ahead and put up the two hundred thousand out of their own pockets.

I did not know one honest man in the whole town.

My father took bribes, thinking they were offered out of respect for his moral calibre. And if boys wanted to be moved into a higher form at school they boarded out with their teachers and paid through the nose. At recruiting time the military commander's wife took bribes from the young men. She was not above accepting a few drinks either, and was once too drunk to get off her knees in church. The doctors also took bribes at call-up time. The town medical officer and the vet levied a regular tax on butchers' shops and restaurants and at the local college there was a brisk trade in certificates granting exemption from military service. The higher clergy took bribes from the lower and from church-wardens. If you applied to the municipal offices, the citizens' bureau, the health centre or any other institution they would shout after you, 'Remember to say thank you', and you would go back and hand over thirty or forty copecks.

Social composition

Towns tended less to be organic growths than in western Europe, and to exist as the result of administrative policy. Catherine the Great set up over two hundred towns in just over twenty years, being persuaded that Russia required a *bourgeoisie* such as it clearly did not possess, but mainly with the intention of strengthening administrative control over her far-flung Empire. It was easy to create a town by decree. 'To transform a village into a town, it was necessary merely to prepare an *izba*, or log-house, for the district court, another for the police-office, a third for the prison, and so on. . . . All this required very little creative effort' (Mackenzie Wallace, i, p. 261). A hundred years after Catherine's death a Russian *bourgeoisie* had indeed come into being, and the usual claim that it was not very numerous is belied by statistics, since about half the urban population consisted of burghers, merchants and members of other bourgeois categories. But it is true that this was not a *bourgeoisie* on the European model and that it was not influential in affairs of state.

A provincial Russian middle-class family, the Ulyanovs of Simbirsk. The boy (bottom right) later became better known as the great revolutionary leader Vladimir Ilyich Lenin. His father, seated next to him, was a school inspector; his elder brother Alexander, standing (centre), was executed in 1887 for taking part in a plot to assassinate Alexander III.

As already pointed out, many town-dwellers were peasants temporarily or permanently absent from their villages. Members of the non-landowning gentry also tended to reside in towns, while landowners themselves often wintered in town, spending only part of the year on their estates. According to the 1897 census the peasants accounted for 38·8 per cent and the gentry for 6·2 per cent of all town-dwellers (Aleksandrov, p. 326). Most of the remainder, 44·3 per cent of the overall urban population, belonged to the estate of the burghers. Though no better translation of the word *meshchanin* suggests itself, it must be added that 'burgher' conveys too solid an impression for a group which excluded merchants, a more prosperous category, and included small traders, owners of apartment-houses, craftsmen, factory workers and indeed more or less anyone who could not be fitted in elsewhere. The burghers had their own communes with elected elders – less vital institutions than the village commune, but by no means ornamental, since they too could exile offending members to Siberia.

Industrial workers

By the end of the century the connection between the Russian factory worker and the village commune, on whose roll he might still be inscribed, had grown tenuous. There was now an increasing number of skilled workers who were also second-generation proletarians. The number of factory workers as a whole may have come to as much as three million by 1900 (see p. 94). Labour conditions were lamentably typical of industrial revolutions in general. Long hours, inadequate and irregular wages, sometimes compulsorily in kind (the so-called 'truck system') at disadvantageous terms from the factory shop, harsh industrial fines for misdemeanours real or fancied, widespread use of child and female labour, inadequate safety precautions – all these were features of the Russian factory. So were vile living conditions in shanty suburbs or factory barracks with several families sometimes crowded into one room, though such factory accommodation was at least usually free. Labour laws, for example those of 1882 and 1897, were passed in an attempt to improve these conditions – by provisions which were, however, often evaded. Trade unions were made illegal under a law of 1874, though in 1902 a high official of the Moscow police called Zubatov founded a special workers' society with activities that included singing patriotic songs and demonstrating in favour of the Tsar. But Zubatov's organisation was by no means entirely a joke. His idea was to improve the workers' lot by non-revolutionary means. Russian workers went on strike many times in the last decades of the century, despite the suppression of unrest by police and mounted Cossacks, and labour troubles reached their most violent pre-1917 peak in the first Russian revolution, that of 1905.

All this is of historical importance, but the Russian industrial worker does not figure prominently in literature of the great age, partly because the great age was nearly over before the Russian worker came into any prominence. Chekhov was aware of the factory-workers' miseries, as is shown in his story *A Doctor's Visit* (1898) and elsewhere, but had no intimate knowledge of the workers' life. So he showed these conditions only from outside, by contrast with his detailed pictures of the urban middle class and of rural Russia.

Among leading Russian writers Maxim Gorky knew the poor of the towns best of all – in fact it was he who popularised the Russian proletariat as a literary theme. But it was not so much factory workers as tramps and petty criminals, for example in the story *Chelkash* (1895) and the play *The Lower Depths*, who were his first main heroes. His story *Twenty-six Men and a Girl* (1899) describes sweated workers in a small bakery. His most celebrated treatment of the factory worker proper is found in his novel *The Mother* (1907), which describes the Russian revolutionary movement, the action being based on the history of Sormovo, a district of Nizhny Novgorod (the author's home town, now renamed Gorky in his honour).

Merchants and businessmen

Gorky's fiction takes in a wide social spectrum, and he has also described the urban *bourgeoisie*. Some of his studies of Russian merchants, including *The Artamonovs' Business*, were, like *The Mother*, published outside the period considered here, but one of the best, *Foma Gordeyev* (1899), was his first novel and describes the wealthy merchant milieu on the Volga.

The merchants (*kuptsy*) formed a special class within Russian society, and they included factory-owners as well as traders, so the term merchant may be misleading and it might be better to call them businessmen. Merchants did not form an estate in the same sense as did the gentry and clergy, since the status of merchant was more precarious. It was not hereditary, but was obtained by paying the dues required to join one of the two (before 1863 three) merchants' Guilds, of which the First Guild was for the wealthier, including those engaged in foreign trade, while the Second was for humbler operators. At the beginning of the twentieth century the First Merchant Guild numbered 30,000 members and the Second about 400,000. If a merchant was unable to meet his dues he would probably revert to being a burgher or peasant.

In contrast to gentry and officials, the merchants belonged with clergy and peasantry to the least europeanised part of the community. They were apt to sport huge beards and have the hair of their heads parted in the middle. The more old-fashioned continued to wear long black double-breasted coats buttoned down the middle in traditional Russian style, whereas gentlemen dressed in the European manner. Merchants did not usually speak any language except Russian. They might even be unable to read or write that, but it could be an expensive mistake to assume that such illiterates were poor businessmen. Many successful merchants were Old Believers, and also clung to the ways of old Moscow by keeping their wives and daughters in comparative seclusion. They liked to dispense hospitality, staging lavish banquets at vast expense with plenty of sturgeon, champagne flowing freely, and with luck a high

Portrait of a merchant's wife,
a Mrs Obraztsov of Rzhev.

official or a general or two among the guests to lend tone. Successful merchants built elaborately appointed houses and spent money on large ornate mirrors, grand pianos which were never played and other costly furniture. But all this was for show. When not entertaining, the host might occupy poky little rooms in some corner of the house with his family.

In the works of Russian literature best known outside Russia, Russian merchants do not figure prominently. One merchant in Russian literature familiar to the foreign theatre-goer is Lopakhin in Chekhov's *Cherry Orchard*, and for a fuller study of the merchant milieu in Chekhov the reader can turn to his story *Three Years* (1895). But the main portrayer of merchants is an author little known outside Russia, though well worth knowing – the playwright Ostrovsky. Merchants also figure prominently in the gallery of Old Believer characters displayed in Melnikov-Pechersky's works. The industrialists of the Urals are described in the works of D. N. Mamin-Sibiryak, including his novel *The Privalov Millions* (1883).

Other categories of town-dwellers

The general category of town-dwellers included, in addition to burghers and merchants, further subdivisions with smaller membership. These were honorary citizens, who might have either hereditary or life status. To this group were assigned for example sons of the clergy who had not entered the church, certain officials, and merchants who had made outstanding gifts to charity. The grade of honorary citizen was introduced in 1832 and conferred exemption from corporal punishment, recruitment and the poll-tax. Yet another estate, which existed in some towns, was membership of one of the craft corporations (*tsekhi*). But by the end of the nineteenth century formal distinctions between all estates were breaking down, and an individual might even not know his own social status until he needed a passport. As this suggests, Russian society was proceeding in the direction taken by western Europe.

Leisure activities

In the disposal of leisure time town-dwellers did not follow the ritual of the countryside, though in small towns the church's influence was almost as strong. But townsmen's opportunities for entertainment were naturally greater, and in the larger cities there were concerts and theatres to be visited. As readers of Russian literature will remember, picnics were a favourite amusement, especially if combined with gathering mushrooms. Muscovites, for example, could drive out to Sokolniki in the north-east of the city where for a few copecks they could have the use of a ready-stoked samovar with which to make tea in the open air, while St Petersburgers could take a trip to the islands or the Gulf of Finland. Country picnics also offered revolutionaries a chance to conspire without being overheard by agents of the secret police.

Town parks often provided bands and a pleasant place to dance or stroll in the evening. There were various bazaars such as Moscow's mushroom bazaar, held in the first week of Lent on the ice

of the Moscow River for the sale of dried and pickled mushrooms. It was also the practice to erect huge toboggan-slides – known, literally, as 'mountains' – which descended from specially built towers. One of these was to be found in St Petersburg between the Alexander Column and the Admiralty, where it was possible to ascend again and proceed on a second slide to Dvortsovy Square. These huge slides were surrounded by trading and amusement booths. For those who found this sort of thing tame and could afford to indulge themselves, there were such things as hectic rides with jingling bells, driven in a fast troika by a *likhach* (a special brand of dare-devil driver) with spirited horses to fashionable restaurants with champagne and choruses of gipsy girls. From such places the dissolute customer might move on 'somewhere else' (*yeshcho kuda-to*) – i.e. to a brothel. In keeping with the character of the two capitals, French or German restaurants predominated in St Petersburg, whereas in Moscow the style was more national and the *traktir* or Russian inn, complete with icon, was the characteristic hostelry.

Two amenities enjoyed by the town-dweller, at least of the more privileged sort, require special comment. The first was the widespread use made of clubs of various kinds. Some, such as the St Petersburg Yacht Club and English Club, were the exclusive meeting place of diplomats, high officials and aristocrats. There

Left. A typical *traktir*, or inn, 1862. At the table on the right a bearded figure is pouring tea, while on the left hookahs and spirits or wine are preferred. The icon in the top right corner is characteristic.
Below. A toboggan-slide in St Petersburg.

were also commercial clubs for the use of merchants. Provincial centres all possessed their gentry clubs and there were often clubs for professional people, small officials and merchants. Clubs might contain a restaurant, a reading-room and a large hall for staging elaborate receptions and balls – such as that described in the provincial gentry assembly hall in Chekhov's *Order of St Anne* (1895). But the main activity, according to literary and other evidence, was gambling over the card-table – often regarded as the main vice of the Russian privileged classes.

Another characteristic urban institution of increasing popularity was the practice of hiring country cottages (*dachi*) not far away from one's place of residence and preferably on a lake, river or sea accessible by railway. To such resorts urban husbands would pack off their wives and children for the summer, often themselves commuting to their place of work at special seasonal reduced fares. The *dacha* husband, a joke figure as one particularly vulnerable to cuckolding, became a staple feature of *fin-de-siècle* funny stories.

One practice not exclusive to Russian society was that of keeping open house on the afternoon or evening of a fixed day each week, when it was possible for friends of the family to drop in without any specific invitation. Hence such information as 'we receive on Thursdays', sometimes dispensed in Russian novels by the lady of the house, who usually took the leading role on social occasions. Such was the practice of polite society, but Russians of all classes were celebrated among foreigners for their hospitality, which erred if at all by its very excess. The celebration of namedays and birthdays of members of the family was one pleasant excuse for dispensing good cheer and another practice confined to urban Russia – as opposed to the village, where it was not much followed.

A fairly violent corrective to any unduly rosy impression of nineteenth-century Russian urban pastimes is provided in much of Gorky's fiction and in such earlier works as Gleb Uspensky's *Manners of Rasteryayev Street* (1866) describing the seamier side of life in his native Tula.

PART FOUR

Law and disorder

13 Officials

The system of control

Imperial authority was enforced by a complex system of pressures and controls, some of which have been indicated already – the use made of the landowning gentry to keep the peasantry in line, and also of the Orthodox Church, conceived by authority as a bulwark of the state and custodian of its ideology.

The system of controls must now be further explored. This involves examining the civil service, law-courts, police and army, and also education, which was constantly under review with the aim of using it to combat revolution and produce malleable citizens. As will be noted, political opposition often reared its head within the very apparatus of control, especially in the law-courts, in the zemstvos, in education and above all in publishing, so this aspect of things must be kept under review, though the opposition is also considered more directly in chapter 18. For the moment it is important to note that imperial Russia was, after all, a going concern, even if its progress was a stumbling and painful affair. It did work, and it is the concern of the present chapter to show how, with particular reference to the imperial civil service.

Variety of officials

Foreign visitors were often struck by the vast numbers of officials who seemed to be found all over the place in imperial Russia, all wearing some kind of uniform, with dark green the dominant colour. Besides civil servants of various kinds, they also included many persons who would not automatically be regarded as functionaries in other societies, but who in Russia held official rank and wore uniforms. Members of the liberal professions were often employed by the state, and so many lawyers, doctors and architects held official rank. So did university professors, who, if sufficiently distinguished, might rate the title Your Excellency like Professor Serebryakov in Chekhov's *Uncle Vanya*. Gymnasium (grammar school) masters, being state employees, also rated as officials, which is why a schoolmaster like Kulygin in Chekhov's *Three Sisters* may appear on the stage in uniform and even introduce himself as a 'court councillor' (see p. 190). Students, such as Trofimov in Chekhov's *Cherry Orchard*, also wore a uniform, though this provision was not in force throughout the period. But the idea that every other Russian was an official of some sort is an exaggeration. The total number of persons belonging to the class was only about one in two hundred and fifty of the population at the beginning of the twentieth century (Schlesinger, p. 60), and they were naturally most thickly congregated in the two capitals where foreigners were likely to notice them.

Officials as seen in literature

The imperial word for official, *chinovnik*, has become a term of abuse in Soviet Russia. If the evidence of nineteenth-century literature is anything to go on, this use of the word is thoroughly justified, for so many Russian authors portray the workings of the imperial bureaucracy as an indecorous farce. The first writer of note to explore the theme thoroughly was Gogol, himself briefly an official in St Petersburg. He produced two especially memorable studies – one comic, the play *The Inspector-General*, and the other tragi-comic, the story *The Overcoat*. Among many followers of Gogol the young Dostoyevsky took up the theme with his wretched Makar Devushkin, hero of his first novel, *Poor Folk*, and with the fantastic twin heroes of his second novel, *The Double*.

A practice puzzling to the uninitiated reader is that of calling civil servants of the first four ranks 'generals', though they might never have donned military uniform or know one end of a gun from another. Civil service generals abound in Russian literature, as the result of which Virginia Woolf once claimed that, in a typical Russian novel, 'we open the door and find ourselves in a room full of Russian Generals' (Woolf, p. 177). Such generals were often comic figures like General Pralinsky in Dostoyevsky's *Nasty Anecdote* (1862), who intrudes on the wedding celebrations

A galley proof
from Tolstoy's novel
Resurrection (1899).

of a subordinate, gets helplessly drunk, collapses face down in a plate of blancmange and has to be put to bed on the nuptial couch. As this episode shows, authors did not always defer to rank when it came to ridiculing the civil service, though by common consent a lowish grade, that of titular councillor (class nine), was the most comic of all. The mere mention of a titular councillor was enough to create pleasurable tension in the reader, who could assume that some kind of slapstick comedy was likely to follow.

But were imperial officials really quite as funny as all that? Herzen did not think so, and he knew the milieu well, having himself been employed as a provincial official during exile to Vyatka and Novgorod. In the following passage, which begins chapter xv of *My Past and Thoughts*, he explicitly dissociates himself from Gogol's exuberant ridicule:

One of the saddest results of Peter the Great's reforms [Herzen writes] is the development of officialdom. It is an artificial, uneducated, voracious class. Totally incompetent ... and wholly ignorant of all except official forms, it is a sort of lay priesthood officiating in law-courts and the police, and sucking the people's blood with thousands of thirsty and dirty mouths.

Gogol slightly raised one part of the curtain and showed us Russian officialdom in all its ugliness, but Gogol unintentionally reconciles us by making us laugh. His great comic talent overcomes his indignation. Besides, being shackled by Russian censorship, he could barely touch on the gloomy aspect of this filthy underworld in which the fates of the wretched Russian people are decided.

Somewhere in those smoke-stained offices through which we hustle, shabby persons are scribbling away on grey paper, then copying on to official stamped paper – and individuals, families and whole villages are injured, terrorised and ruined. A father goes into exile, a mother to prison and a son into the army, and it all bursts on them unexpectedly as a clap of thunder.

One unsavoury practice of provincial officials, touched on by Herzen, was that of blackmailing and terrorising vulnerable groups – minority peoples (especially Jews) and Old Believers and

что то, что из хлѣба
и вина, несмотря на эти ку-
... вѣрить въ то, что изъ
... въ рот... такъ, что... и
вызывая плачущаго мальчика... было вино съ
хлѣбомъ ... правдивое убѣжденіе ... при-
... дѣйствіе ...

Долженъ ... его спрашивать, гово-
рить ли объ этомъ ... Наконецъ священникъ го-
ворилъ, какія-нибудь ... что дѣла-
... надо

... принеся дары какъ-то ... вращая
... клавиши, крестился и строго
взглядывалъ на арестантовъ, когда замѣчалъ какой-нибудь
... Когда стали причащать дѣтей, онъ вынес-
... и самъ соотвѣтственно подалъ мальчика, кото-
раго причащалъ и подержалъ его, пока Христа ... Большинство же арестантовъ уже совершенно не знало не
только смысла того, что дѣлалъ за перегородкой священникъ, но хотя бы приблизительно о томъ, что предпо-
лагалось, что дѣлалось въ этомъ богослуженіи. Они вѣрили только тому, что то, что происходило передъ ними,
было выраженіемъ единственной настоящей вѣры.

Впереди всѣхъ женщинъ стояла арестантка этой
той женщины, которая, въ этой крестьянской одеждѣ въ
тюрьмѣ, шла служащею въ Сибирь. Она дѣвочка полу-
тора года была на рукахъ у матери. Эта еще ничего
не понимала и не глядя молилась. Но два мальчика
пяти и трехъ лѣтъ, благоговѣйно, ровно только-только
старушекъ, какъ перегибая-стоящимъ, въ подкрѣ-
... съ ними ... правильно должны склады-
лись на ноляхъ, когда другіе становились, и не пере-
ставая крестились и кланялись въ земли. Мальчики эти
были твердо увѣрены въ томъ, что то, что они дѣлали,
очень важно и разливалось потому что убиваютъ то дѣлать,
и вспытывали пріятностъ, глядя на освѣщенный золотомъ
... неожиданно и иконы, на важной священника и
слушая его торжественные возгласы и пѣніе хора ... худо-
жественное наслажденіе.

То же ... возвышенное состоянiе взрослыхъ
арестантовъ. ... считали все это поповскимъ зо-
... но ... какъ ... клавялись...
усердно крестились...

... эту вѣру, которая пре-
подавалась имъ этимъ богослуженіемъ ... что то, что про-
... которую надо вѣрить, которая для чего
нужна, и во время можетъ пригодиться.
... будетъ хорошо, а если же мы... и не вѣрить, то можетъ случиться что-нибудь дурно...
Такъ вѣрю большинство, но были и такіе, которые
вѣрили даже въ то, что надо вѣрить, а только находи
... нѣкоторое удовольствіе въ томъ, чтобы стоять въ...
... арестантами о Маслова...
... надо радоваться ... войти въ первую...
... смотрѣлъ... священника, одежду...

Once a provincial vice-governor, later a radical editor, M. Ye. Saltykov-Shchedrin (1826–89) wrote many works satirising Russian officials. His *History of a Certain Town* describes a sequence of absurd governors and the town itself, Glupov, was put forward as a symbol of imperial Russian administration as a whole.

sectarians, who were the victims of legal discrimination. Here the discretion open to local officials in interpreting complex and self-contradicting regulations could be a powerful weapon of extortion.

Herzen's protest against excessive use of ridicule in portraying officials reminds one that not all officials in leading works of nineteenth-century fiction are ludicrous. For example, Anna Karenin's husband is an impressively serious study of a former provincial governor occupying a senior post in St Petersburg. Tolstoy clearly disapproves of Karenin and his activities, both official and unofficial, but treats him with a certain respect – even though his sticking-out ears, dry, civil servant's manner, habit of cracking his fingers and false jocularity seem to have been expressly created to antagonise his small son and provoke his attractive wife into committing adultery. In his later novel *Resurrection*, Tolstoy handles the upper reaches of the bureaucracy more roughly than he had in *Anna Karenin*, but makes his officials seem dangerous and heartless rather than ridiculous. Other serious character studies of officials include that of Kalinovich, hero of Pisemsky's *A Thousand Souls*, whose rake's progress includes a period as a provincial governor. There is also an excellent portrait of a St Petersburg official – the dry, ironical, card-playing Orlov – in Chekhov's *Anonymous Story* (1893).

Herzen's protest against the use of ridicule was heeded not at all by Saltykov-Shchedrin, supreme chronicler of the Russian bureaucracy. He was himself an official for a longer period than Gogol or Herzen, rising to a provincial vice-governorship, so that he knew his subject exceptionally well. His *History of a Certain Town* (1869–70) is outstanding among his many studies of grotesque officials. It describes a series of ridiculous governors, and the imaginary town Glupov (from *glupy*, 'stupid') is put forward as a symbol of the imperial administration as a whole.

Among the points scored against officials in literature, sycophancy towards those of higher rank, as in Chekhov's early *Fat and Thin* (1883), is prominent. But the most common accusation is that of taking bribes. As Chekhov stated in his savage description, quoted in the previous chapter, of the unnamed provincial capital in *My Life*: 'If you applied to the municipal offices, . . . the health centre or any other institution they would shout after you, "Remember to say thank you", and you would go back and hand over thirty or forty copecks'. It has been argued in defence of these exactions that civil servants were badly paid and that bribery, pretty well in accordance with a fixed tariff, had become a traditional way of supplementing inadequate incomes. The dishonest official was not the one who took bribes (since that was absolutely normal), but the one who hung on to a bribe when he could not perform the service for which it had been paid, or who would not stick to the usual tariff – like one of Gogol's officials, accused of taking bribes 'above his station'.

Ranks, honorifics and awards

The official class was a creation of Peter the Great, who in 1722 set up the celebrated hierarchy of fourteen official grades, termed the table of ranks, which remained in force with few alterations until 1917. These ranks had cumbrous titles borrowed from Prussian and other western European models, and care is needed in translating them from Russian. 'Privy councillor' is, for example, a tempting rendering for *tayny sovetnik*, and is in fact adopted below for want of a better alternative, but can give a misleading impression in English. The fourteen ranks were as follows:

Class	Civilian Rank	Military Equivalent (after 1884)
1	Chancellor	Field Marshal
2	Actual Privy Councillor	General
3	Privy Councillor	Lieutenant-General
4	Actual State Councillor	Major-General
5	State Councillor	
6	Collegiate Councillor	Colonel
7	Court Councillor	Lieutenant-Colonel
8	Collegiate Assessor	Captain
9	Titular Councillor	Staff Captain
10	Collegiate Secretary	Lieutenant
11	Ship's Secretary	
12	Provincial (*gubernsky*) Secretary	Sub-Lieutenant
13	Provincial (*provintsialny*) Secretary	
14	Collegiate Registrar	

Of the above, classes eleven and thirteen fell into abeyance in the first half of the nineteenth century, and the military rank of major, formerly equivalent of collegiate assessor, was discontinued in 1884.

Each official had an appropriate honorific title with which he was addressed by subordinates and on official occasions. Classes one and two above were 'Your Supreme Excellency'; three, four and five rated as 'Your Excellency'; six to eight inclusive were 'Your Supreme Honour' and the remainder 'Your Honour'. Wives enjoyed these honorifics too, whence the occasions on which Anna Karenin is referred to as Her Excellency.

Among the preoccupations of Russian officials was the award of various decorations called orders for which they might from time to time qualify. Most of these had several different grades, like that of St Vladimir with its four classes, even the lowest of which (class four) conferred hereditary membership of the gentry on the recipient. The order of St Anne (with three classes) was slightly less exalted – after receiving his St Anne class two, the hero of Chekhov's *Order of St Anne* planned to move on to the St Vladimir ladder and was rash enough to hint as much by making an execrable pun to the local provincial governor when, in accordance with etiquette, he paid a call to thank His Excellency for the award. Other orders included the four classes of the military order of St George, awarded for outstanding bravery, and the orders of St Stanislaus (three classes), which formed the humblest category of those granted to civilians. Less commonly encountered in literature are: the order of St Andrew (one class only), given to members of the imperial family and the highest of the orders; the order of the White Eagle (one class); of Alexander Nevsky (one class); and of St Catherine (for women, two classes).

Higher governmental organs

As already indicated, even the most exalted governmental organs had the function of executing the sovereign's will rather than of initiating policy. This is true of four bodies which must now be mentioned. The Senate was originally set up by Peter the Great in 1711 to supervise the whole administration and as the chief legislative, administrative and judicial organ. Its actual powers fell far short of this, especially in the period studied here, having decreased notably in the 1810s with the institution of the ministries (which were formally subordinate to it) and of the Committee of Ministers. But from 1864 onwards the Senate did operate as an effective court of appeal besides discharging numerous minor functions. The Committee of Ministers functioned from 1802 to 1906 with the task of co-ordinating the work of different departments. Its capacity was mainly advisory, as was that of the Council of State, set up in 1810 to discuss, but not initiate, prospective legislation. A similar role was fulfilled by a shorter-lived body, the Council of Ministers, which met at the Tsar's discretion and under his presidency between 1861 and 1882.

The ministries, establishment of which was completed in 1811, played an important part in the administration. These have been described as 'state departments of the usual west-European type, each with a well-defined competence and each under the direction of a minister who was personally responsible for the legality of his actions' (Karpovich, p. 18). To this must be added a reminder that ministers were appointed and dismissed as and when the Tsar saw fit, and that he could take their advice or not as he wished.

At the end of the nineteenth century the following ministries were in existence: foreign affairs; war; internal affairs; justice; finance; agriculture and state properties; transport; education. To these eight must be added the administration of state horse-breeding and a body called state control with the task of auditing government income and expenditure. The ministries were all administratively subordinated to the Senate and department of state control, but there were also various offices directly responsible to the Tsar: the ministry of the imperial court; his Majesty's personal chancery; his Majesty's personal chancery for the institutes of the Empress Mariya (responsible for orphanages and girls' schools). There was also an imperial chancery for dealing with petitions.

The ministries maintained staffs of varying size and structure, according to their own particular needs, in the provinces as well as in St Petersburg. Thus the provincial gendarmerie or security police (after 1880), together with provincial postal, telegraph and censorship officials, came under the ministry for internal affairs, and the ministry of finance maintained provincial offices for tax-collecting purposes. The other ministries too had sizeable provincial establishments.

Provincial administration

Provincial governors, in their capacity as representatives of the central government, exercised general supervision over all local officials and were more directly responsible for some in their capacity as representatives of the ministry of internal affairs. So the provinces were by no means starved of bureaucrats, as the many works of literature devoted to provincial officialdom illustrate.

For purposes of administration the Empire was divided into territorial units, of which there were one hundred and one in all at the end of the nineteenth century. These consisted chiefly of the provinces (*gubernii*), of which there were seventy-eight and of regions (*oblasti*), of which there were eighteen and which may be considered for practical purposes as being provinces under a different name – they were in fact areas remote from the centre or possessing unusual social institutions. Provinces and regions differed greatly in size and density of population, their average area being greater than that of the smaller European states such as Belgium or Switzerland. The population varied from a few hundred thousand to just over four million, and some of the largest in area were smallest in population. With the vast, sparsely inhabited Yakut Region in eastern Siberia (population at the end of the nineteenth century just under three hundred thousand, at less than one person per ten square kilometres) may be contrasted, at the other end of the scale, Kiev Province, with one eightieth of the area of the Yakut Region, but with a population fourteen times as great.

Each province and region came under the administrative control of its governor, who was appointed by the central government. The governor had his residence in the provincial capital (*gubernsky gorod*), which usually gave its name to the province as a whole – thus: Tula Province, Vladimir Province. But some provinces, for instance Podolia and Volhynia, had names not deriving from those of their chief towns. Provinces were subdivided into smaller units termed districts (*uyezdy*), each with a district capital (*uyezdny gorod*) as its administrative centre. There might be about eight districts within a typical province. Districts did not have governors, but came under the general administrative control of a chief of police, the so-called *ispravnik*.

In some areas several provinces or regions were grouped

together in general-governorships under governor-generals, who as the name implies, exercised military as well as civil authority At the end of the nineteenth century there were nine such general governorships – all on the periphery of the Empire, mainly in places where there seemed to be a need for stricter control than could be imposed by a distant central authority. These were Finland; the Kingdom of Poland; the Caucasus; also (in European Russia) the South-West and North-West Territories; (in Siberia) Irkutsk and Amur; (in Central Asia) Turkestan and the Steppe. In addition to the above, the city of Moscow itself had a governor general – a compliment to its status as the old capital.

As well as the provinces and regions there were four city administrations responsible directly to the central government. These were those of St Petersburg, Odessa, Sevastopol and Kerch-Yenikale, each of which came under a town captain. And to complete the tally, the island of Sakhalin enjoyed the status of department (*otdel*).

Local government

It will be remembered that the reforms of Alexander II included provisions for a new kind of local government, that of the zemstvos (rural councils) instituted by a law of 1864, and also of town councils (*gorodskiye dumy*) instituted by a law of 1870. These bodies were elective, albeit on a complex system with heavy weighting in favour of the gentry and of property owners. The zemstvos existed both on provincial and district level, having their headquarters in provincial and district capitals. Their members, elected for periods of three years, in turn elected executive boards, also for three years, to manage current business. Provincial councillors were elected by district councillors, and they also elected executive boards. The town councils had a similar organisation, being elected for four years and forming an executive board, and they also chose a mayor. Thus alongside state officials were functioning officials of a different kind – unpaid, self-consciously public-spirited and the repository of the hopes of liberal-minded Russians, who saw in these new institutions a school of practical democracy.

The rural councillors often saw themselves in this light too. So, unfortunately for them, did the central authority, which proceeded to hamper them in various ways. They did not even exist in all provinces, for by the end of the century they were functioning in only thirty-four. And the 'counter-reforms' of Alexander III included a law of 1890 limiting their power and increasing their dependence on the state. They were in any case impeded by various powers of near-veto exercised by provincial governors, by the ultimate control of the ministry of the interior and by the difficulty of levying adequate taxes to meet their requirements. They were also compelled to accept the local marshal of the gentry (of district or province as the case might be) as chairman, thus confirming the gentry's dominant position. Still, peasants did find their way on to the councils, and incidentally often showed themselves more conservative than the representatives of the gentry on whom the government relied to keep them under control.

The councils were largely concerned with local economic needs – with the upkeep of roads and bridges, anti-famine precautions, medical care and elementary schools. By the end of the century they were employing many teachers and doctors, among whom they attracted the more radical-minded. Attempts by the councils to exercise wider political influence, outside the confines of local affairs, were carefully watched and thwarted by central authority. A certain tension existed between the local councils with their new, progressive traditions, and the state officials, though the latter were by no means all the hidebound reactionaries of popular mythology.

14 Crime and punishment

Judicial reform

The overhaul of the judicial system, enacted in 1864, is widely considered the most effective among the many reforms of the period. There was much room for improvement, since justice had previously been administered according to a complex and cumbrous system by judges dependent on the administration, badly paid and operating in secret at wearisome length, evidence all having to be taken down in writing.

Class distinctions were also reflected in the treatment which a citizen might receive at the hands of the law. Writing in the period preceding the judicial reforms, Herzen stated:

> To know the real meaning of Russian prisons, courts and police, you have to be a peasant. . . . Political prisoners, who mostly belong to the gentry, are strictly confined and savagely punished, but their fate is not at all to be compared to that of the unhappy bearded ones [the peasants]. . . . Such is the chaos, brutality, arbitrariness and perverseness of the Russian law-courts and police, that an ordinary person . . . does not fear punishment so much as the process of the law. He waits impatiently to be sent to Siberia, his martyrdom ending with the beginning of his punishment.
>
> (*My Past and Thoughts*, ch. x.)

The new system introduced in 1864 was based largely on the French and to some extent on the English model. Procedure was simplified and made public. It was arranged for judges to be properly paid and hold their appointments permanently unless they should themselves be convicted of a crime. They thus became less dependent on the administration, though not entirely independent, for threats of transfer to a less attractive neighbourhood and other pressures could still be applied to keep them in line. Trial by jury was introduced for more serious criminal cases, and barristers with clearly defined qualifications and their own professional association made their appearance. The new system operated under the passive supervision of the Senate, which maintained cassation departments as courts of appeal empowered to order re-trial, and under the more active supervision of the ministry of justice, which maintained a representative, the public prosecutor, in each of the newly constituted county courts (*okruzhnyye sudy*) to act as prosecuting counsel in criminal trials.

The reformed courts became, as had literature itself, an outlet for freedom of speech otherwise denied public expression. Russian advocates, like the public prosecutor at Dmitry Karamazov's trial in *The Brothers Karamazov*, were often carried away by eloquence on topics not relevant to the issues before the court. And, as Dostoyevsky often complains in his journalistic articles, Russian juries were excessively tender-hearted, even going so far as to acquit prisoners who had pleaded guilty. An instance of this occurred in 1878 when a revolutionary, Vera Zasulich, was acquitted by a jury after shooting and wounding General Trepov, town captain of St Petersburg, who had ordered the flogging of a political prisoner. The episode inspired Turgenev's *Threshold*, one of his *Poems in Prose* (1879–83), in which he invokes a female revolutionary.

The new courts

County courts were introduced gradually from 1866 onwards, and their jurisdiction normally extended over a province. Appeal from their decisions could be made in the first instance to the appropriate chamber of justice (*sudebnaya palata*), with jurisdiction over several provinces. County courts and chambers of justice were for more serious offences. Minor matters (involving civil disputes over a sum less than five hundred roubles, and criminal cases in which the penalty did not exceed a three-hundred-rouble fine or one year's imprisonment) were to be adjudicated by justices of the peace elected by district zemstvo assemblies. In these courts procedure was informal and fatherly – a contrast to the relative pomp of the county court with its three uniformed judges (the president in the centre) and barristers in frock-coats. From justices of the peace appeal was made in the first instance to the district assembly of justices of the peace. But the jurisdiction of justices of the peace was much reduced with the institution in 1889 of land captains, who took over their functions in the country-side. And town courts, with judges appointed by the ministry of justice – not elected, as were the justices of the peace – replaced them in many urban areas. By the beginning of the twentieth century the so-called peace courts were operating only in Moscow, St Petersburg and six other large towns.

It must also be borne in mind that the peasants, some three quarters of the population, were after emancipation subject to trial in minor cases by cantonal courts consisting of fellow-peasants, often illiterate. These enforced peasant law based on custom and dealt with petty theft, family disputes and so on. In addition to these, military courts judged offences committed by military personnel and also, as shown below, certain offences committed by civilians. Ecclesiastical courts tried divorce cases and those involving the discipline and professional interests of the clergy. There were also special commercial courts in certain cities of the Empire.

Police

The governor of each province was also the head of the police within the province, and it will be remembered that at district level the chief of police, the *ispravnik*, was also head of the district administration as a whole. For police purposes districts were sub-divided at the next level down into units called *stany*, each consisting of several cantons. The chief of police for a *stan* was the *stan* prefect (*stanovoy pristav*), below whom came a number of (usually) mounted policemen called *uryadniki* – the office was introduced in 1878 in order to quell increasing rural unrest. At the lowest level peasants termed 'hundredsmen' and 'tensmen', responsible to the *uryadnik*, were elected to discharge the most menial police duties, on a part-time basis, and the village elders also carried out certain quasi-police functions. Large towns had a different police organisation under special chiefs of police.

The above remarks apply to the ordinary police. There was also a special security or political police, distinguished by blue uniforms and called the gendarmerie. During the existence of the Third Section of the Imperial Chancery, from 1826 to 1880, the gendarmerie was controlled by the head of the Third Section, and after 1880 it was transferred to the ministry of the interior, which already controlled the ordinary police. Secret agents and *agents provocateurs* reinforced the work of the uniformed gendarmerie and had the task of penetrating revolutionary conspiracies, and for the security apparatus as a whole the colloquial term *okhrana* ('protection') was often used. The gendarmerie was, incidentally, also responsible for policing the railways – hence the occasional presence of a gendarme on station platforms in Russian fiction.

Uniformed or secret, ordinary or political, policemen were mistrusted and despised by the average citizen – to an extent which that prudent Scot Mackenzie Wallace did not appreciate at the beginning of his investigations into nineteenth-century Russia. Having cannily equipped himself with a document from the gendarmerie to certify that during his travels round Russia he was not engaged on any nefarious activity, he soon found that presentation of it only made him the object of immediate suspicion to any decent citizen (Mackenzie Wallace, i, pp. 318–9).

Investigators

In 1860 the investigation of criminal cases was taken out of the hands of the frequently brutal police and entrusted to special investigators called examining magistrates (*sudebnyye sledovateli*), who were made more or less independent of police and public prosecutors, and were at first intended to enjoy permanent tenure of office. In practice the ministry of justice soon found it prudent to appoint them on a temporary basis to make them more amenable. A memorable fictional investigator is Porfiry Petrovich in

Dostoyevsky's *Crime and Punishment*, who uses 'psychological' methods to induce the murderer Raskolnikov to confess.

Two fictional trials

Two fictional murder trials are especially noteworthy – that of Dmitry Karamazov in Dostoyevsky's *Brothers Karamazov* and that of Catherine Maslov in Tolstoy's *Resurrection*, which begins when the prisoner is brought from gaol to face her judges in a county court. *Resurrection* provides an especially full picture of legal and penal procedure, including descriptions of the hearing of an appeal to the Senate, of prison conditions and of transportation to Siberia. The novel is set in the 1880s, by which time the new courts were a little less new than they had been, and Tolstoy's satirical description was a sharp corrective to any undue optimism about the reformed judiciary. Readers can also ponder the fact that Dmitry Karamazov and Catherine Maslov are both victims of judicial miscarriage.

Penalties

Capital punishment was abolished in 1753, except for the murder or attempted murder of a member of the imperial family. But this provision was evaded in various ways. It was possible to award so many strokes of the knout that death was likely to follow. The use of the knout was banned early in the reign of Nicholas I, and that of the birch by a law of 1863 – not the least welcome of Alexander II's reforms – abolishing the severest forms of corporal punishment. After this measure flogging could, however, be administered to delinquent peasants on the orders of cantonal courts. It could also be imposed in disciplinary units of the army, and on prisoners and deportees to Siberia for disciplinary offences.

With regard to political offenders, Vera Zasulich's acquittal (see p. 197) incensed the authorities, and henceforward care was taken to see that such cases did not come before juries. A special court had already been set up in St Petersburg in 1872 to try cases of treason, besides which wide use was made of powers of exile and other punishment by so-called administrative procedure – that is, without trial and on the decision of officials.

Military courts retained the power to impose capital punishment, and thus political conspirators and assassins, of whom there were so many in the last decades of the monarchy, became liable to execution. This was assisted by declaring throughout large areas of the Empire states of emergency, whereby such offences were tried by military courts and not by the ordinary courts, which had no power to impose the death sentence.

It will be remembered that the Decembrist poet Ryleyev and Lenin's elder brother Alexander were among nineteenth-century Russians who were executed, and that Dostoyevsky narrowly escaped this fate, only to suffer a variety of other penalties. His *Notes from the House of the Dead*, in effect an account of his four years in gaol at Omsk in Siberia, is a classic of Russian penal literature and it is a pity that he has not left a similar account of his months in the fortress of St Peter and St Paul in St Petersburg before trial. On release from gaol, Dostoyevsky was compelled to serve as a private in an army unit, another common form of punishment, and was gradually permitted the privileges of promotion, demobilisation, residence in European Russia – and finally of residence in St Petersburg which he had quitted ten years earlier.

As Dostoyevsky's penal history reminds one, fortresses and monasteries were available as places of incarceration in addition to ordinary prisons. The fortress of St Peter and St Paul had an especially distinguished roll of nineteenth-century inmates, rivalled by that of the Schlüsselburg fortress, also on an island in the Neva. Monasteries conveniently equipped with dungeons included the remote Solovetsky on islands in the White Sea, and the handier Suzdal monastery, about a hundred and forty miles from Moscow.

Sentence to Siberia took two forms, of which the more severe was termed *katorga*, sometimes misleadingly translated 'hard

The convict barge *Irtysh* on the River Ob, showing prisoners taking the air in the cage constructed on deck. Political prisoners and gentlemen would usually be segregated from the rank and file of convicts and housed in surroundings which were slightly less uncomfortable. Sometimes the others might all be stowed below while a few of the gentry got a breath of air in the cage.

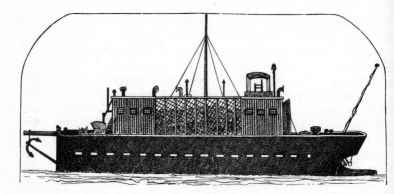

labour'. Hard labour, for example in the notorious silver mines of Nerchinsk, might or might not be involved, but what *katorga* (originally meaning 'galley') did imply was confinement in gaol with the status of convict. Even when the sentence had been served, compulsory permanent exile to Siberia followed. As a milder punishment, exile without convict status was commonly imposed on people termed 'exile-deportees' (*ssylno-pereselentsy*).

The impact of exile, though less than that of *katorga*, did vary a great deal. Being banished temporarily to a family estate in the country as an administrative measure, as happened to Turgenev and Pushkin, was the least uncomfortable kind of exile. In extreme cases exiles might have to eke out existence under the eye of a local policeman somewhere in the Yakut Region. Hard though the life might be, such exiles (in the case of political prisoners) were usually members of the gentry with independent means, or were paid a small subsistence allowance by the government. They were often treated as social superiors by the local inhabitants and might be free to receive and write books, and to correspond with friends. Like Herzen when exiled to Perm and Vyatka, they might also be able to take their valets along.

Enormous distances and a savage climate made Siberia a difficult

A convict in Siberia. It was customary to crop convicts' hair close and to shave one half of the head entirely. Convicts wore a sort of dressing-gown with a device on the back like an ace of diamonds, and fetters on their ankles, joined by a chain.

place to escape from, but the attempt was often undertaken successfully. It was common for Siberian peasants to leave food and drink outside their houses for the benefit of escapees. This was done partly out of sympathy, for the common people thought of convicts as the 'unfortunate' or 'unlucky' ones, but it was also a form of insurance because such desperadoes were less likely to break into a hut if they could find food and drink outside it.

The number of persons imprisoned and exiled for political reasons was tiny, if comparison is made with the scale of persecution operated by twentieth-century totalitarian states, and the sufferings of convicts in general hardly compare with those of later concentration camp victims. But conditions were horrible enough. The trouble was not so much systematic brutality as fearful overcrowding in transit prisons, prison barges and permanent gaols, where stink, filth, prevalence of epidemic disease and high mortality were the features that impressed observers. Convicts often had half their heads shaved, wore fetters on their ankles and a sort of dressing-gown with a device on the back like an ace of diamonds. The political prisoners among them were kept under especially close supervision. Visiting the penal colony of Sakhalin in 1890, Chekhov was allowed free access to all prisoners except the 'politicals', and *Sakhalin Island*, his study of penal condition based on these experiences, is an impressive work both from a scholarly and literary point of view. As it reminds one, the imperial authorities made no bones about calling political prisoner political prisoners, for it was not then thought necessary, as in more recent times, to pretend that persons persecuted for political reasons had committed some non-political offence.

Whether in prison or exile, political offenders enjoyed a surprising degree of freedom to read and write. Chernyshevsky himself not only wrote *What is to be done?* in the fortress of St Peter and St Paul, but also did a great deal of other writing and translation there and in Siberia. It was in the same fortress that Pisarev spent about four and a half years and wrote his most influential work. P. G. Zaichnevsky actually composed the manifesto *Young Russia*, one of the most inflammatory clandestine revolutionary pamphlets of the 1860s, while in a Moscow gaol, where his cell was turned into a sort of discussion club for university students who came and went more or less as they wished There was at least one instance of an imprisoned revolutionary being permitted to leave his cell under a soldier's escort in order to buy political literature in a St Petersburg bookshop. Later in the century Lenin, exiled between 1897 and 1900, was able to complete his *Development of Capitalism in Russia* and to indulge in large-scale journalism in southern Siberia. As all this shows, the policy of causing political opponents to disappear without trace was not followed by the imperial government.

15 The army

In political and social life

The armed forces were an important pillar of the imperial Establishment, not least because of the tradition of appointing army generals to high administrative office. The army figures prominently in literature, Lermontov, Tolstoy and Dostoyevsky all having served as officers, though the last-named seems to have done his best to forget the fact and was certainly one of nature's civilians. The imperial navy is less prominent in nineteenth-century literature, as it was in Russian life, but one important literary work associated with it in the period considered here is Goncharov's *Frigate Pallas*, based on his experiences as civilian secretary to a governmental mission to Japan in 1852–4 headed by Admiral E. V. Putyatin.

Though the Russian army in the first half of the nineteenth century was in many ways a backward and cruel institution, it also showed gleams of liberalism. Only perhaps in a land of surprises such as imperial Russia might one find guards officers, of all people, in the vanguard of a movement for reform. Yet this is what happened during the period of subversive secret societies which preceded the Decembrist revolt of 1825. The campaigns following Napoleon's invasion of Russia in 1812 had opened the eyes of Russian soldiers serving in western Europe to the backwardness of their own country, showing them that forms of government other than the autocratic did exist elsewhere.

A Russian guards regiment, the Semyonovsky, had mutinied in 1820. Yet the guards were just as much of a social *élite* in Russia as elsewhere, 'quite fit to be compared with the German in the social position of their officer corps', as one authority states (Schlesinger, p. 361). But officers of less smart, non-guards regiments, normally dependent on their meagre pay, could not cut such a dash. One may contrast Lieutenant-colonel Count Vronsky, lover of Anna Karenin and owner of race horses and vast estates, with the less resplendent Lieutenant-colonel Vershinin, the battery commander in Chekhov's *Three Sisters*, who had an unpresentable

wife with suicidal tendencies and spent all his life 'knocking around from one lot of rooms to another, with a couple of chairs and a sofa and stoves smoking all the time'.

In literature

Pushkin's work includes descriptions of the Russian army in the late eighteenth century at the time of the Pugachov rebellion – *The Captain's Daughter* and *History of the Pugachov Rebellion*. And, as mentioned above, his *Journey to Erzerum* describes his own adventures as a camp-follower to the Russian army during war against the Turks in 1829. Lermontov went a stage further than the civilian Pushkin by obtaining a commission in the Hussars in 1834, and made an army officer, Pechorin, the 'Hero of our Time' in his novel of that name. Dostoyevsky trained as a cadet in the sappers, and though he soon resigned his commission, was later compelled to serve with the army in Siberia as part of his punishment for political misdemeanours. But he made scant use of his army experiences in fiction.

Much use was made of the army as literary copy by Tolstoy, who saw active service as an officer. His descriptions start with

Far left. Tolstoy in 1855 when he was serving in the Crimean War.
Left. Dostoyevsky in army uniform in 1858. Dostoyevsky got his schooling
as a sapper cadet in the St Petersburg Army Engineering School. Later, after
serving four years in the convict prison at Omsk, he was made
to rejoin the army. It was remarked at his cadet school that
Dostoyevsky looked out of place ('like a seminarist') in uniform.

early stories, *The Raid* (1853) and *The Wood-felling* (1855), reflecting his experiences in the Russian army in the Caucasus during the
years 1851–4. Tolstoy also saw active service at the siege of
Sevastopol during the Crimean War, and made use of it in his
Sevastopol Stories (1855–6). He later delved back into earlier
martial history with his epic of the Napoleonic campaigns, *War
and Peace*.

Duels fought in defence of marital or regimental honour, reck-
less gambling, exciting love affairs and alcoholic orgies are among
the features that lend glitter to the life of the Russian officer in
nineteenth-century Russian fiction. There was another aspect to
the officer's life, as Tolstoy himself did not conceal, and for an
account more concentrated on the seamy side of the mess and less
likely to stimulate recruiting than Tolstoy's, readers could turn to
Kuprin's *The Duel* (1905).

The pre-reform army

Reading much of Russian fiction about the army, one may tend to
lose sight of the 'other ranks', whose conditions of life, especially
in the first part of the nineteenth century, were unenviable. Conscription was on a class basis, gentry and clergy being exempt, as
were also merchants on payment of a special tax. Thus conscripts
were drawn from the peasantry and from the lower ranks of townspeople – craftsmen and burghers. Young peasants dreaded the
prospect of having 'their foreheads shaved', as happened to those
unlucky enough to be selected as recruits. This was regarded
almost as the prelude to a lingering death, owing to the harshness
of conditions in the army and to the fact that the term of service
in the ranks was fantastically long – normally twenty-five years
until after the Crimean War, when it was reduced to fifteen,
among other relaxations which formed a preliminary to the conscription law of 1874 described below. A soldier's wife became for
all practical purposes a widow. Yet in spite of all disadvantages it
was sometimes possible for a conscript to buy a substitute.

Punishments for disciplinary offences were brutal. They included flogging and running the gauntlet, whereby the victim was dragged between ranks of fellow-soldiers, who were compelled to beat him with switches of willow as he passed along what was known colloquially as 'the green road'. The number of blows inflicted might run into several thousand. After a mutiny at Staraya Russa in Novgorod Province in 1831, inspired by a rumour that soldiers were being deliberately infected with cholera by the authorities, a prolonged orgy of knoutings, floggings and beatings ordered by Nicholas I led to well over a hundred deaths among some two thousand six hundred mutineers who were punished (Riasanovsky, *Nicholas I*, p. 14). Running the gauntlet, as still practised some twenty years later, is described with horrible vividness in Dostoyevsky's *Notes from the House of the Dead*.

Reform

Conditions were greatly improved by the army reforms of General D. A. Milyutin, who was minister of war from 1861 to 1881. In the law of 1874 he took the class bias out of conscription, to which all male citizens over the age of twenty-one now became liable, though in peace time it was not usually necessary to call up more than about a third of them, and certain categories – including the clergy, only sons and men who had brothers with the colours – were exempt. The period of active service was reduced to six years followed by a number of years in the reserve and militia. Further concessions gave advantage to those who had attended school and university. Thus university students were liable to only six months with the colours, while ex-pupils of the gymnasiums and other secondary schools need only serve eighteen months or three years, and pupils of primary schools need serve four. For university and secondary school graduates who cared to enlist voluntarily rather than take their chance of not being conscripted, the above terms were halved.

The army became a place where peasants first learned to read and write, for Milyutin was successful in putting army education on a sound footing. Discipline was made less harsh, corporal punishment being now confined, at least in theory, to penal units, though it was no uncommon thing even after the reforms for an officer to strike a soldier. Conditions remained bad by absolute standards, but the situation had been transformed by Milyutin's reforms if comparison is made with the early part of the century.

Chekhov was sympathetically disposed towards the Russian army. According to Stanislavsky, he sent his own military representative to supervise the rehearsals of *Three Sisters*, in which army officers figure so prominently. Chekhov wanted his officers shown as 'charming, decent people', not as blimpish heel-clickers. If Stanislavsky is to be believed, he also used to become lyrical about the cultural mission performed by the Russian army when posted to remote parts of the country, to which it took 'knowledge, art, happiness and joy' (*The Oxford Chekhov*, iii, pp, 314–6).

Like so much else in life, the Russian army had its good and bad sides, and the bracket between them, as befits the 'broad Russian nature', was especially wide.

16 Education

General development

The progress of nineteenth-century Russian education follows the pattern of imperial development in general by showing fairly impressive improvement on modest beginnings. Thus all educational facilities had greatly expanded by the end of the century. For instance, in 1899 the Empire had nine universities with about 17,000 students, whereas back in 1809 there had been a mere 450 students in four universities (Florinsky, ii, p. 726; Kovalevsky, p. 482; these figures do not include the non-Russian universities of Helsingfors and Vilna). On the other hand, imperial education is less impressive if compared with that offered by the advanced countries of western Europe in the same period. An eloquent figure reflecting educational backwardness is the high proportion (seventy-four per cent) of citizens of the Empire between the ages of nine and forty-nine recorded as illiterate in the 1897 census.

Authors as pupils

The variety of Russian education can be shown by considering how some leading writers fared in youth. As befitted representatives of the upper crust, Turgenev and Tolstoy were instructed at home by private tutors, though Turgenev did briefly attend a preparatory school in Moscow and was taught to read Russian by an amateur, his father's valet. Wealthy gentry families like these generally employed resident tutors and governesses, who were often French, British or German and thus equipped to provide small Russians with oral practice in foreign languages. In his *Childhood*, to some extent a fictional account of his own early years, Tolstoy describes a German tutor, called Karl Ivanovich Mauer, who is modelled on his own real-life tutor, Theodor Rössel. Rössel was succeeded as Tolstoy's tutor by a Frenchman, St Thomas, who appears in *Childhood* under the name St Jérôme.

Turgenev and Tolstoy became university students aged fifteen and sixteen respectively, for in the first half of the century the age

The great actor and director Konstantin Stanislavsky (1863–1938), a photograph taken in 1880 showing him in the uniform of a gymnasium pupil. The gymnasiums, which may be thought of as Russian grammar schools, provided the best institutional schooling at all widely available.

for entering the university was low by modern standards. Tolstoy went to the University of Kazan, where he read oriental languages for a year, then switched to jurisprudence, but failed to take his degree. Turgenev attended three universities. He did one term at Moscow before going to St Petersburg, where he graduated in 1837 after three years in the history–philology faculty, then attended the University of Berlin for a time, returning to St Petersburg to begin reading for an M.A. degree with which he did not persist. All this, together perhaps with his honorary degree at Oxford (1879), entitles him to be called the most academically involved of the great Russian writers, but not the most erudite – Tolstoy, who pursued knowledge so devotedly in so many fields, surely deserves that honour. Tolstoy also gave more attention than any other leading Russian writer to the theory and practice of education itself.

Pushkin did not attend a university, but received the most exclusive of institutional upper-class educations available to

Chekhov's student card entitling him to attend courses in the medical faculty of Moscow University in the first semester of the academic year 1880–1. He continued occasional practice as a doctor long after he had made his name as a writer.

Russian boys at the Imperial Alexander Lycée at Tsarskoye Selo, the Tsar's residence near St Petersburg. He joined this establishment in the year of its foundation, 1811, and left in 1817. This was a boarding-school with a preliminary class and a six-year course, of which the first three years provided general education and the last three a legal and 'political' training. The school was designed to produce high functionaries, but also turned out to be a nursery of poets, of whom Pushkin was the most illustrious. He retained happy memories of years at the lycée, later commemorated in his lyrics. After leaving school he became an official of the ministry of foreign affairs, but did not last long in what was a most unexacting position.

Pushkin's near-contemporary Gogol also failed to attend university and also became an official in St Petersburg after leaving his school – another well-known lycée, that of Nezhin in the Ukraine. He had ambitions to shine as an administrator, but his civil-service career was brief, as was his later tenure of a professorship at St Petersburg University from 1834 to 1835. Turgenev was one of his students and has described how the new professor missed two out of every three lectures, spoke inaudibly, seemed highly embarrassed, and when conducting the final examinations in his subject, sat with a handkerchief wrapped round his face and refused to ask the candidates any questions.

Dostoyevsky had an education ill suited to his temperament. After being a pupil of private schools in Moscow as a young boy, he trained for five years as a cadet at the Military Engineering School in St Petersburg, passing out in 1843 with an army commission which he resigned in the following year. He had managed to combine military training with wide reading of imaginative literature, often devoured in the watches of the night.

Education of a more conventional type for a writer was received by Chekhov, who attended the gymnasium (grammar school) at Taganrog where Greek and Latin formed a large part of the curriculum. This was a most respectable form of education by the standards of the day, and Chekhov, though no outstanding pupil, was able to proceed to the University of Moscow. There he qualified as a doctor and unofficially as a writer by stories and sketches published during his student years.

Gorky received little formal education, being taught to read by the cook on a Volga steamer for whom he worked as pantry-boy. Of this skill, once acquired, he made good use, besides receiving a rough but thorough education in the 'university of life'. He ironically gave the title *My Universities* to the section of his autobiography devoted to what would have been his student years if he had succeeded, as he had hoped, in gaining admission to the University of Kazan.

Universities

The first Russian university and also the one with the largest nineteenth-century student body was that of Moscow, founded in 1755 (4,407 students in 1899). Herzen, who was a student there in 1829–33, says that Moscow University had become more and more the focal point of Russian education, since it had all the necessary conditions for development: 'historical importance, geographical

214

position and the absence of the Tsar' (*My Past and Thoughts*, ch. vi).

The University of Derpt, in what is now Estonia, had an especially complex history. Originally a Swedish foundation in 1632, it was closed in 1710 and reopened by Alexander I in 1802, the language of instruction being German from then until 1895 when it became Russian, the name Derpt having been officially changed back to the town's original Russian name, Yuryev, as part of the drive to russify the periphery of the Empire. To add to these complexities the German name for Derpt is Dorpat and the town is now called Tartu.

The year 1804 saw the foundation of Kazan and Kharkov Universities. In 1819 St Petersburg University was founded, followed by those of Kiev (1833), Odessa (1864), Warsaw (1869) and Tomsk (1888). A step in the other direction was the closing of the University of Vilna in 1832. With minor variations each university had four faculties: history and philology; physics and mathematics; law; and medicine. St Petersburg had, in addition, a faculty of oriental languages (transferred from Kazan), but no medical faculty, the deficiency being supplied by the St Petersburg Military Medical Academy. Derpt had a fifth faculty, of Lutheran theology. For the higher education of the Orthodox clergy there were four clerical academies (*dukhovnyye akademii*) independent of universities: those of Kiev, Moscow, St Petersburg and Kazan.

Women were not admitted as university students, but were provided with what was in effect university education by 'higher women's courses' started in Moscow in 1869, and also established in St Petersburg, Kazan and Kiev in the 1870s. A Women's Medical Institute was established in St Petersburg. Like other liberal features of the educational system, facilities for women's education were severely curtailed under Alexander III. University autonomy also suffered during the recurring periods of political oppression. In the freest periods the highest official of each university (the rector), the deans of the faculties and the professors were elected within the universities themselves. But during periods of reaction these officials were directly appointed and dismissed by the ministry of education, or at least such appointments had to be officially ratified. In the early years of the nineteenth century the universities had even exercised control over the secondary and primary schools in their area, but this right was taken away from them.

After the Crimean War, and increasingly during the rest of the period under review, Russian universities became centres of political unrest. This was the age of student demonstrations, riots and strikes, supported by the more liberal university teachers, who risked dismissal by such displays of sympathy. Peasant disturbances at the time of emancipation and the Khodynka disaster of 1896 (see p. 105) were among occasions evoking student protests. Worse riots followed in St Petersburg University in 1899, sparked off by an official warning that unruliness would not be tolerated during the University's annual celebration on 8th February. A student demonstration was dispersed by mounted police with whips, after which a general strike of students was declared and carried out in many other universities too. Student demonstrators were liable to harsh treatment, being sent down from the university in large numbers and often drafted into the army as privates – the deferment or curtailment of military service, to which they were entitled as students, conveniently lapsed when they were expelled. But this sort of thing only inflamed the situation, and in 1901 a former student assassinated the minister of education, N. P. Bogolepov, thus carrying academic protest to its ultimate limit.

Student unrest was due to political dissatisfaction aggravated by specific grievances, such as the disciplinary powers exercised by university inspectors and a virtual ban on free corporate activities. Many students were poor, as is not unknown in other countries, and they often lived in squalor, as does the student Raskolnikov in Dostoyevsky's *Crime and Punishment*. Even Raskolnikov was better housed than many of his fellow-students, for at least he did not have to share his miserable garret in St Petersburg with anyone else.

Another well-known representative in literature of Russian university life is Peter Trofimov, the 'eternal student' in Chekhov's *Cherry Orchard*. There are references in the dialogue to him 'already having been sent down from the university twice', and 'having been landed in some pretty queer places', from which it seems clear that Soviet commentators are not being entirely fanciful when they claim Trofimov to have been conceived by Chekhov as a budding revolutionary. To portray him as such was impossible under censorship conditions of the time, as Chekhov implied in a letter to his wife: 'You see, Trofimov is in exile off and on, and gets chucked out of the university every so often, and how is one to depict that sort of thing?' (Letter of 19th October 1903).

Educational policy and organisation

So far as educational policy is concerned, a period of relative liberalism corresponding to the reign of Alexander II was sandwiched between two slices of intolerance in the reigns of Nicholas I and Alexander III, followed by some relaxations in the first part of Nicholas II's reign and considerably more after 1905. But things were not quite so simple as that. During most of Alexander II's reign – from 1866 to 1880 – the minister of education was an extreme reactionary, Count D. A. Tolstoy, whose views on education had little in common with those of his more famous namesake the novelist. D. A. Tolstoy's tenure of office did see a big increase in the number of schools and of the pupils attending them, but he kept a firm grip on appointments and syllabuses, particularly those of the gymnasiums (grammar schools). A feature of his policy was the emphasis laid on the study of Greek and Latin as a means of curbing political unrest. It was thought that concentration on these classical languages, especially on their syntax, might nip revolutionary sentiments in the bud – a vain hope because the gymnasiums in fact became centres of political disaffection, like the universities which many gymnasium pupils would later attend.

Chekhov, the only nineteenth-century Russian writer of the very front rank to complete a full course at a gymnasium, never turned into a political firebrand, but was left with a distaste for Greek and Latin which apparently lasted him for life. Classicists may take some comfort from the fact that Chekhov, who received the most intensive classical education among leading Russian writers, also wrote exceptionally disciplined and elegant Russian prose, though how much credit for this can be given to the model of Cicero and Demosthenes is not clear. In his *Man in a Case* (1898) Chekhov has a brilliant description of a repulsive gymnasium teacher of Greek whose only pleasures in life are interfering with his colleagues' activities and rolling the Greek word *anthropos* round his tongue.

One aim of educational policy-makers in periods of political reaction was to make it impossible for pupils of humble social origin to enter the gymnasiums and universities. Increases in school and university fees, and insistence on irksome formalities were used from time to time to discourage lower-class children from claiming places in these establishments, which should be the monopoly of the gentry according to the more diehard social engineers. An official circular issued in 1887 proclaimed the need to keep out of the gymnasiums such undesirables as the children of coachmen, footmen, cooks, laundresses, small shopkeepers and similar people. This came out nearly ten years after Chekhov had received his leaving certificate from the Taganrog Gymnasium – otherwise he, being the son of a struggling shopkeeper, might have had to seek his schooling elsewhere.

For the administrative purposes of the ministry of education the Empire was divided into educational areas (*uchebnyye okruga*), of which there were twelve at the end of the nineteenth century. High officials called curators (*popechiteli*) were responsible within a given area for all educational institutions coming under the ministry, including universities, gymnasiums and primary schools. The general pattern was for each area to be centred on a single university, the curator's office being in the university city of his area.

Secondary schools

Despite attempts to use dead languages as a political narcotic, the gymnasiums did on the whole provide the best schooling widely available. They were first developed on any scale under Alexander I, when the initial aim was to provide every provincial capital with its gymnasium. By the end of the century this modest plan had been overfulfilled, and there were nearly two hundred gymnasiums in all. The gymnasium course was pretty well uniform throughout Russia, and had been expanded from four years to eight. Unsatisfactory pupils were kept down to do a second year in the same form – as happened to Chekhov in both the third and fifth forms – because of an inadequate performance in the annual examinations, a dreaded event. There were also pro-gymnasiums – similar institutions, offering the first part, four years, of the gymnasium course. Then there were also modern schools (*realnyye uchilishcha*). These placed emphasis on mathematics, science and modern languages, and they gave entry to technical colleges, whereas the gymnasiums proper provided their graduates with entry to the universities and preferential access to civil service posts. The above were all boys' schools, but girls too had their gymnasiums, being better served with secondary school education than they were at either university or primary level. Girls' gymnasiums offered a seven-year course with an extra year for those who wished to qualify as schoolmistresses. They also inflicted less Latin and Greek on their pupils.

The church maintained its own secondary schools – the seminaries mentioned above (p.148). Their programme followed similar lines to that of the gymnasiums, but also included a mass of additional theological material designed to fit pupils to serve the Orthodox Church. There were fifty-five seminaries in 1900 with some 18,000 pupils. The church also maintained diocesan girls' secondary schools, mainly for daughters of the clergy. They were designed to fit girls to become priests' wives and were not academically ambitious. In 1900 there were over sixty of them with about 15,000 pupils.

Primary schools

As may also be remembered, the church maintained church schools on a primary level. These offered a four-year course designed for, but not exclusive to, children of the clergy. They must not be confused with the much more numerous parish (*tserkovno-prikhodskiye*) schools, which were administered by the church for the population at large, forming a sizeable part of the Empire's primary school system. Schools of literacy (*shkoly gramoty*) on a lower level still, also came under the Holy Synod, which was administering nearly thirty-five thousand primary schools of all types, with well over a million pupils, at the end of the nineteenth century.

In the same year the overall tally of primary schools throughout the Empire was nearly eighty thousand, with a total of nearly four million pupils. There was only one authority with wider control over primary education than that exercised by the Synod – the ministry of education itself, responsible in 1896 for some two-fifths of the Empire's primary schools with nearly two-thirds of the pupils. At the same time the ministry of war was responsible for over ten thousand primary schools with some three hundred thousand pupils (for figures in this and preceding paragraph, see Kovalevsky, p. 476 ff).

Schools were set up by village communes, by town councils and also by the zemstvos, the zemstvo schools being of particular importance by the end of the nineteenth century. Many schools were founded by private individuals, including writers, and that established at Yasnaya Polyana by Tolstoy in 1859 became especially famous. A noted theorist of education, as of almost everything else in human life, Tolstoy also liked teaching peasant children and produced a fairly successful reading primer, his *ABC Book*, in 1872. Chekhov too founded schools for the peasants during his residence in the village of Melikhovo, south of Moscow, and his story *My Life* illustrates the sort of difficulties which this might involve.

Other schools

Besides the institutions mentioned above, Russia also possessed a variety of boarding-schools including the quaintly named 'pensions for well-born spinsters' for daughters of the gentry. There were Sunday schools designed to teach, not religious knowledge but reading and writing, and officially suspected as hotbeds of revolutionary agitation. And there were increasing numbers of technical and vocational colleges, including the Moscow Higher Technical School. It also became a common practice for factories to provide schools for the children of employees.

Even by the end of the period considered here, this rapidly growing system was on too small a scale for the gigantic Empire. With her large proportion of illiterates, Russia was still a long way from achieving universal primary education by 1904. And that of girls was particularly neglected. In 1896 less than a quarter of the overall number of primary school pupils were girls. No wonder that, according to a favourite proverb of the (male) Russian peasant: 'A woman is long on hair and short on brain'.

7 Press and censorship

Importance of the press

Since almost all writings of value first appeared in a periodical (see p. 33 above), the literary situation cannot be fully understood without some knowledge of the press and of the workings of censorship. This is also necessary for a general understanding of Russian intellectual life and of the political conflict which smouldered beneath the surface or flared up openly throughout the period. Although so many types of publication were subject to censorship, the press provided the most important – at times the only – arena for public debate and for the struggle between the forces of imperial 'law' and liberal or revolutionary 'disorder'.

Periodicals

The most important vehicles for new literary works were 'fat journals', the name by which Russians refer to their bulky reviews, mainly monthlies. Besides printing original Russian literature, these published literary criticism and translated foreign literature, and also philosophical and historical material. Social and political problems had to be handled in a very roundabout way, especially under Nicholas I, but these were the topics that really mattered to many readers and editors.

In the first half of the century the monthly reviews had more influence than the daily or weekly press. This was partly because of the difficulty, at a time of harsher censorship, of reporting and commenting on day-to-day political events, which hampered newspapers and weeklies more than monthlies. It was also due to poor communications. In rural districts the post was not delivered to the house, but had to be collected, often from a considerable distance. It would not usually arrive more than once a week and might be delayed by blizzard, flood or cholera quarantine. The monthlies could afford to look at Russian and world affairs in a more leisurely way than their flimsier competitors and so had an advantage. Through them intellectually alert Russian country squires – and there were not a few – could keep abreast of cultural trends.

By the 1880s there were about a dozen of these reviews being published, with circulations rising to nine or ten thousand each. It was possible to keep a review going on a subscription list of only a few thousand, and they had influence out of all proportion to their readership, partly because the proportion of intellectuals in the population was so small. And more freedom of speech could be exercised in the monthlies than in any other public medium except for books – more leniently censored, but less immediate in impact.

The freer conditions under Alexander II opened the press to less muffled political discussion and a new social phenomenon appears on the Russian scene – the newspaper campaign. War news began to boost the importance of the daily newspaper at the time of the Crimean War (1853–6), and patriotic press campaigns were fought against the Poles during the Polish revolt of 1863, and

Contributors to *The Contemporary*. Sitting
(left to right): Goncharov, Turgenev, Druzninin,
Ostrovsky. Standing: Leo Tolstoy, Grigorovich.
The journal was a museum of literary
talent as well as a source
of political and social fireworks.

against the Turks before and during the Russo–Turkish War of 1877–8.

Even in the grim days of Nicholas I a periodical could have a political slant. The notorious *Northern Bee* (St Petersburg, 1825–64), edited by F. Bulgarin, was for a time the only daily newspaper entitled to receive political information, being almost an organ of the government, since it was largely controlled by the Third Section of the imperial chancery. Other periodicals kept up some sort of political opposition, and the best known of these was *The Contemporary*.

The Contemporary and *Notes of the Fatherland*

The Contemporary had been founded by Pushkin, but its period of greatest influence began in 1846, when it was bought by Nekrasov. For a short time before his death Belinsky was the chief literary critic there, and later critics and social theorists among contributors included Dobrolyubov and Chernyshevsky. *The Contemporary* published most of Turgenev's *Sportsman's Sketches* from 1847 onwards, and his first two novels, *Rudin* and *A Nest of Gentlefolk*. It also first published Tolstoy's *Childhood*, *Boyhood* and *Youth*. *The Contemporary* was closed in 1866 in the wave of restrictions following the attempt on the Tsar's life in that year. Nekrasov now went over to *Notes of the Fatherland* (St Petersburg, 1839–84), which had published Belinsky's early critical works, Goncharov's *Oblomov* and two early novels of Dostoyevsky, *The Double* and *The Village of Stepanchikovo* (1859). In 1875 Dostoyevsky returned to *Notes of the Fatherland* with his long – and extremely bad – novel *A Raw Youth*.

M. N. Katkov and *The Russian Herald*

As the last-mentioned episode shows, Nekrasov was no match for the conservative publisher and journalist M. N. Katkov when it came to cornering the best new novels. It was Katkov's review.

The Russian Herald (Moscow, 1856–87; Moscow and St Petersburg, 1887–1906) that first published all four of Dostoyevsky's greatest novels: *Crime and Punishment, The Idiot, Devils* and *The Brothers Karamazov*. With those four on his pages, Katkov could well afford to let an inferior work like *A Raw Youth* go. His review also brought out three of Turgenev's four last novels (*On the Eve, Fathers and Children* and *Smoke*) as well as *War and Peace* (in part) and *Anna Karenin* (Parts One to Seven). Thus nine of the ten most significant works of Russian fiction published between 1860 and 1880 all first appeared in this one review. The exception was Turgenev's *Virgin Soil*, published in the *Herald of Europe* (St Petersburg, 1866–1918).

Katkov has not always had credit for these *coups*, perhaps through disapproval of his political views. In Mirsky's *History of Russian Literature*, for example, *The Russian Herald* does not even rate a mention, though there is much information on *The Contemporary* and *Notes of the Fatherland*. But Katkov showed great tact in nursing such a 'difficult' author as Dostoyevsky and was a notable literary impresario. He could, by the way, be something of an autocrat himself when he disapproved of an author's material. He refused to print Part Eight of Tolstoy's *Anna Karenin* because he deplored Tolstoy's scathing attitude to the Russian quarrel with Turkey, and it was he who banned the 'banned chapter' in Dostoyevsky's *Devils* where Stavrogin confesses to the rape of a little girl. So Katkov sometimes exercised his own political or moral censorship.

Other publications

After Katkov's death in 1887 there were no major novels to scoop and new names appear among the journals which printed leading literary works. Chekhov's career shows a writer working his way up from the bottom of the ladder. He began in a trivial comic weekly, *The Dragonfly* (St Petersburg, 1857–1908) and then published in other minor organs such as *Alarm Clock* (Moscow,

1873–1917) and the weekly *Fragments* (St Petersburg 1881–1916) before graduating upwards by way of two newspapers, the *St Petersburg Gazette* and the influential conservative *New Time* (St Petersburg, 1868–1917). Then came his début in the 'fat journals' when the monthly *Northern Herald* (St Petersburg 1885–98) published his long story *Steppe* in 1888, after which Chekhov remained a 'fat journal' man for life. He published in many, but it was the liberal monthly *The Russian Idea* (Moscow, 1880–1918) that produced the bulk of his longer and better-known stories, including *Ward No 6* (1892), *An Anonymous Story*, *Three Years*, *Peasants* and *The Lady with the Dog* (1899). An apolitical animal, Chekhov happily published in all shades of the press from the conservative *New Time*, an unfashionable platform for an author who wished to impress the Russian intelligentsia, to the Marxist *Life* (St Petersburg, 1897–1901), though he gradually moved leftwards in his choice of vehicle. *Life* incidentally published Gorky's two earliest novels, *Foma Gordeyev* and *Three of Them* (1900–1). The latter was not printed in full in *Life*, but was cut off in mid-career when the review was banned in June 1901.

The censor's task and problems

Imperial Russian thought-control was mainly negative. The authorities tried to suppress subversive notions, atheistic, revolutionary and so on, but were less concerned to inculcate improving ideas. They were more eager to keep unwanted matter out than to ram official ideology down readers' throats. It was a censorship of morals, as well as of politics and religion. Even such a modest writer as Chekhov was often forced to suppress details about the sexual relations between his characters (and also to tone down domestic quarrels) so that his stories might be suitable for 'family reading'.

In general Russian nineteenth-century censorship was relatively insensitive in the realm of ideas, being more concerned with matters of fact and with personalities. Varying in severity, but nearly always a nuisance, it hampered writers, editors and publishers, their plans being continually wrecked by officials who were themselves often to be seen tripping over their own red tape.

Absurd examples of censors' interference are often quoted, such as the ban on the phrases 'forces of nature' and 'free currents of air', and the insistence (to deter would-be assassins?) that Roman emperors always 'perished', and were never 'killed'. Musical scores were suspected of cloaking sinister cyphered messages, and one censor even objected to a poet calling a woman's smile 'heavenly' because he thought that no woman deserved such high praise (Rozenberg, p. 40).

The censor's own lot was not a happy one. At one time a special committee was set up to censor censors, giving them a taste of their own medicine. A censor could be punished for lack of vigilance, a very Russian concept, and could be arrested and clapped in the guardroom like a mere author. Censors often objected to harmless material just to show that they were alert. They could be dismissed or suspended, as happened to the censor Boldyrev who let Chaadayev's *Philosophical Letter* into the Moscow *Telescope* in 1834. The censor who passed Turgenev's *Sportsman's Sketches* was dismissed too. So the job was no sinecure. Still, some writers were prepared to take it on and police their own colleagues, the best known being Goncharov, whom one can scarcely see in the role of watchdog of imperial authority or indeed of anything else. The poet Tyutchev and the critic and thinker Konstantin Leontyev, both extreme conservatives, also worked as censors.

Penalties

Disciplinary measures included warnings, reprimands, rebukes, fines, confiscations of offending periodicals, exile, police surveillance and – a typical feature of Nicholas I's reign – detention in the guardrooms of local military garrison units. Isolated words and phrases might be cut or whole paragraphs, items and editions banned. Publications were often closed down. For example, in

1834 the fortnightly *Moscow Telegraph* (Moscow, from 1825) was banned for printing an unfavourable review of a patriotic play, *The Hand of the Almighty Saved the Fatherland*, by N. V. Kukolnik. In 1836 the fortnightly, later weekly, *Telescope* (Moscow, from 1831) was banned for printing the first of Chaadayev's *Philosophical Letters*, in which Russian civilisation was denounced. In 1866, as noted above, Nekrasov's *Contemporary* was closed down. And *Notes of the Fatherland*, to which Nekrasov went over in 1868, was itself closed down in 1884. The Marxist journal *Life*, which published much of Gorky's early work, was banned in 1901 as noted above (p. 225).

Left-wing publications were not the only ones to suffer. Conservative and slavophile organs were also liable to interference, as were those with no definite political slant. In 1863 Dostoyevsky's review *Time* (started in 1861) was closed because of an article on the Polish rebellion, wrongly interpreted by officials as an attack on government policy. Dostoyevsky then started a new review called *The Epoch*, but this had to be discontinued in 1865 because he had lost his readership, and he now faced financial ruin. Reviews could also be crippled by less drastic means, for instance by a ban on advertising, often a main source of revenue.

Pre-reform censorship

Russian censorship was a child of the nineteenth century, though interference, often by the church, had been common before. Vague censorship regulations were brought in under Catherine the Great, in whose reign two leading writers, Radishchev (in 1790) and Novikov (in 1792) were imprisoned and exiled, the former being sentenced to death, commuted to ten years' Siberian exile, in connection with his book *A Journey from St Petersburg to Moscow*. A beginning had been made. But it was not until 1804, early in the reign of Alexander I, that the first comprehensive censorship statute was enacted. Under the new Tsar censorship was at first easy-going, but grew harsher and became especially so under Nicholas I. It was at its most severe from 1848 to 1855, the age of terror by censorship, as it came to be called.

Strangely enough it was in these years that the flourishing realist movement arose – at the very time when, according to the contemporary memoirist A. V. Nikitenko, the number of officials engaged in censorship exceeded the total number of volumes published in a year (Rozenberg, p. 54). Nikitenko was a censor himself, and so knew what he was talking about. Among the bodies censoring or controlling literature at various times between 1804 and 1855 were the ministry of education, the military authorities, the church, the universities, the Second and Third Sections of the imperial chancery, the ministry of transport, the ministry of police, the railway authorities, the commission supervising the building of St Isaac's Cathedral in St Petersburg and even the administration of state horse-breeding. In effect almost any government department could interfere with the printed word, and it was really a wonder that anything got into print at all.

Pushkin and the censorship

One martyr to censorship was Pushkin. After he had been released in 1826 from exile to his family estate at Mikhaylovskoye, Nicholas I said that from now on he would act as Pushkin's personal censor. Pushkin was pleased, thinking that he could go ahead and publish his newly completed verse drama, *Boris Godunov*, but before long he was told off by the Chief of Gendarmes, Count Benckendorff, just for reading the unpublished play aloud in Moscow literary circles without first submitting it to the Tsar. Then it turned out that the special relationship between Pushkin and the Tsar was just an extra encumbrance because Pushkin was to remain subject to the regular censorship as well. And the wretched Benckendorff and his Third Section were to be intermediaries, forwarding the poet's work to the Tsar with their own comments attached.

Russia's greatest poet was required to accept these nuisances as a mark of imperial favour. He even had to receive literary advice from the most august quarter when the Tsar through Bencken-dorff commented on *Boris Godunov*: 'I consider that Mr Pushkin's aim would be fulfilled if, along with *necessary expurgation*, he would change his comedy into a historical tale or novel, similar to Walter Scott's' (letter of 14th December 1826). Pushkin replied frigidly: 'I have received with profound gratitude Your Excellency's letter informing me of His Majesty's most gracious comment on my dramatic poem. I agree that it resembles a historical novel more than a tragedy, as the Sovereign Emperor has deigned to observe. I am sorry that it is beyond my power to recast what I have once written' (letter of 3rd January 1827). Pushkin's play was ready for the press in 1826, but it was not until 1831, and then as a special favour so that he could meet expenses connected with his marriage, that he could publish.

Among many works which could not be published for years because of censorship, or were mutilated by censorship before they did appear, were two political poems of Pushkin's youth: *Freedom* (written 1817; first published in Russian in London in 1856; first published in Russia in 1906) and *The Village* (written 1819; first published in truncated form in Russia in 1826; first published in full in Russian in London in 1856; first published in full in Russia in 1870). Pushkin's long blasphemous poem *Gavriiliada* was written in 1821, but first published in London in 1861.

Other victims

Other works to suffer included Griboyedov's *Woe from Wit* and Lermontov's poems *The Demon* and *Death of a Poet*. Pisemsky's novel *Boyarshchina* (written in 1845, published in 1858) and Chekhov's short play *On the High Road* (submitted for censorship in 1885 and published posthumously) were both banned as too gloomy. From Tolstoy's novel *Resurrection* a scene satirising the Orthodox church service was among no less than five hundred alterations imposed by the censorship, and a full version of the novel did not appear until 1936. Dostoyevsky's most important short work, *Notes from Underground* (1864) was ruined, he said, by 'those swine of censors' who 'banned the section where I deduced the need for a belief in Christ' (letter of 26th March 1864). The missing passage was not restored by Dostoyevsky and has been lost. Then there was also self-censorship, such as is bound to occur in an atmosphere of excessive control over literature. This can seldom be proved to have occurred, but it went on all the time. One instance which can be documented concerns Chekhov, who wrote that his story *My Life* (1896) was 'bound to make a mutilated impression [despite the fact that cuts imposed by the censorship had later been restored when the story appeared in book form] as when I wrote it I could not forget for one moment that I was writing for a magazine subject to censorship' (*Chekhov: Literaturnoye nasledstvo*, p. 213).

The reformed censorship

From 1804 to 1865 censorship was basically preventive, which meant that all material must be submitted for approval to one or more authorities before publication. But it was also punitive – that is, a censor's prior approval was no guarantee at all that objections would not be raised later. With the accession of Alexander II in 1855 censorship was applied more liberally in the atmosphere of impending reform, and in 1865 new regulations were introduced. They remained in force for forty years, though they were called temporary.

The main effect was to whittle down preventive censorship. All original books of ten or more printed pages, and all translated works of twenty or more printed pages, could now be printed without being submitted for prior approval. So could publications of learned societies, and editions or translations of ancient Greek and Latin literature, for even these had been liable to be mutilated or 'corrected' under Nicholas I.

Under the new regulations periodicals were more strictly censored than books – which is why Chekhov, for example, sometimes reconciled himself to cuts imposed on work published in the periodical press, knowing that he could later restore his text when he came to publish it in a book. But here too things were made easier, preventive censorship being partly suspended. Periodicals were now allowed to choose between preventive and punitive control, and the latter, though it sounds more forbidding, actually left them freer. But this provision applied only to the St Petersburg and Moscow press, preventive censorship remaining mandatory in the provinces. This is one reason why the periodicals of the two capitals were able to keep their position of cultural and intellectual leadership.

Censorship was mainly exercised by the ministry of the interior after 1865, but church censorship continued to function and there was a special and irksome theatrical censorship. Though censors had become less troublesome, publications still came in for much interference, which naturally fluctuated according to changes in the political climate. Under Alexander III, as might be expected, conditions were severe. Censorship remained an obstacle to the free development of Russian literature, unless an irksome and clumsy yet not quite crushing system of official control may actually be a stimulus.

Evasive tactics

Elaborate official regulations often provoke elaborate devices for evading them. Russian censorship was no exception, and so in spite of attempts to stop them, writers still found ways of communicating. One technique was indirect allusion in 'Aesopic' language, a term invented by the satirist Saltykov-Shchedrin. The method did not necessarily involve the use of fables, as the name Aesop implies, for any suitable indirect statement would do. When it came to taking a hint and reading between the lines, the intellectually hungry Russian reader was an expert.

Censorship was also evaded by clandestine circulation of manuscripts. Documents circulating in this way included Griboye-

232

Title page of Herzen's magazine *The Pole Star*, published annually by his Free Russian Press in London (1855–62) and in Geneva in 1869. The device in the centre shows the profiles of the five Decembrist leaders hanged on 25 July 1826.

dov's play *Woe from Wit*, which was being passed from hand to hand for five years before it was performed or published. Even after publication, it continued to be passed round because the first published version contained only the woe, according to one contemporary. The wit had all been censored out (see Monas, p. 184). Lermontov's *Death of a Poet* was also handed round in this way. So were many of Pushkin's poems including his *Village*, *Freedom* and *Gavriiliada*, and other famous documents including Chaadayev's *Philosophical Letter*, much of Tolstoy's theoretical work and Belinsky's open letter to Gogol, which became a manifesto of the radical opposition. Handling such material could be dangerous, as Dostoyevsky found when sentenced to death for reading out Belinsky's letter, amongst other things.

Evasion took other forms too. There was the habit of denouncing political articles in the foreign press, with lavish quotation so as to give them publicity in the only way possible. Like other evasive techniques followed under the Tsars, this subterfuge has survived into modern times. Russian periodicals were sometimes published abroad to be smuggled into Russia. The first important example was *The Bell*, published in London by Herzen and Ogaryov from 1857 to 1865, then in Geneva for two years. The same editors also brought out an annual, *The Polar Star*, in London from 1855 to 1862.

Foreign matter

The fate of foreign works on Russian soil was erratic. One surprising import was Karl Marx's *Capital*, which no censor detected as a Trojan horse. The first volume appeared in Russia in Russian translation in 1872 before it had been translated into any other language. But works by Herbert Spencer and Darwin, and even by Heine and Flaubert, were banned or mutilated.

Foreign books and periodicals imported into the Empire in their original languages were censored by a special organ, the 'foreign censorship'. This had branches in Moscow and St Petersburg where foreign material was scrutinised for passages offensive to the Russian government, and these were then laboriously deleted. According to a British observer of these proceedings: 'With a preparation of gutta-percha and powdered glass he [the Moscow censor of foreign printed matter] will cleanse and purify *The Times* of a paragraph, or *Punch* of a joke, in so neat a manner that not a vestige of printer's ink shall remain' (Edwards, p. 32).

18 The opposition

Varieties of disaffection

In the present chapter a closer look will be taken at elements of disintegration and political opposition in imperial Russian society. These cannot be fitted into a tidy pattern. The Empire's internal opponents had no common platform, but differed from each other in all sorts of ways – most significantly in the degree of their addiction to violence. At one end of the scale were advocates of liberal reform, though it is worth remembering that the word liberal had a different resonance in the nineteenth century to that which it has since acquired – the phrase 'a dangerous liberal' did not then seem to be a contradiction in terms, as it might now. At the other extreme were dedicated political assassins, heroes to some and monsters to others. They included the five young people who were publicly executed with extreme inefficiency by a drunken hangman in the Semyonovsky Square in St Petersburg for killing Alexander II with home-made bombs.

Though opposition to the autocracy came chiefly from the political left wing, there were also diehard conservatives who were horrified by Alexander II's reforms. They did not want to see the serfs freed or flogging abolished, and were sometimes called 'planters' by radical journalists who were apt to compare serfdom in Russia with slavery in the United States. As will be remembered, the same decade saw the end of both.

Not all landowning gentlemen were 'planters'. For example, in 1862 the gentry of Tver sent a formal petition to Alexander II asking for political rights to be given to the entire people (they were willing to renounce their own privileged position), and thirteen of them, who later put their names to a more outspoken document on the same lines, were imprisoned for a time. These were actions in favour of liberal reform by members of the gentry acting corporately. As will be remembered, individual gentlemen were also prominent as theorists and practitioners of reform and revolution throughout the century, being well to the fore both as oppressors and oppressed.

For left-wing Russian oppositionists many different terms are used: liberals, progressives, radicals, socialists, populists, nihilists, anarchists, revolutionaries, marxists, communists and terrorists. Some of these terms overlap with and fuse into each other, being neither interchangeable nor mutually exclusive. Specific illegal political parties and conspiratorial groups (such as Land and Freedom and the Socialist Revolutionary Party) must also be taken into account, besides which such important concepts as those of the intelligentsia and slavophilism have to be considered as well.

Westernists and slavophiles

Two main currents – those of westernism and slavophilism – must be distinguished in Russian social and political thinking. The split between the two occurred in the early 1840s. Westernists were those who claimed that Russia was essentially European and that she should learn from and imitate western Europe. The greatest Russian critic, Belinsky, was a leading westernist, as also were the radical thinkers Chernyshevsky, Dobrolyubov and Pisarev. Another was Bakunin, the founder of modern political anarchism, who originally formed a model for Turgenev's Rudin. After protests by sympathisers of Bakunin, Turgenev changed his portrait to the point where Chernyshevsky conceded that it was no longer even a recognisable caricature of Bakunin (Turgenev, *Sobraniye sochineny*, ii, pp. 313–4), and it is true that Rudin in his final form does indeed seem pale beside the ebullient Bakunin. Westernists also included T. N. Granovsky, a liberal professor of history at Moscow University who served as the (admittedly rather remote) prototype for Stephen Verkhovensky in Dostoyevsky's *Devils*. Stephen, father of the nihilist villain Peter Verkhovensky, is very much a figure of fun in the novel, and also stands condemned by Dostoyevsky, who tended to lump liberals and revolutionaries together. Each suffered from the same disease, so what matter if one had it in a milder form, when both were equally dangerous

sources of infection? Dostoyevsky thus dissented from the common practice of contrasting the 'fathers' of the 1840s with the 'sons' of the 1860s, and lumped the two together.

Readers of Turgenev's *Smoke* will remember that the clash between Russian westernists and slavophiles is a major theme in the novel. Since the slavophiles supported the principle of autocracy, there is a tendency to think of them as part of the imperial Establishment, a point of view not at all shared by Nicholas I's censors and police officials. Though the slavophiles were by no means revolutionaries, the very fact that they included notable original thinkers made them an object of official mistrust, especially under Nicholas I when the very act of expressing an opinion, even in support of the government, aroused official suspicion. The slavophiles advocated the emancipation of the serfs and differed from the westernists in their assessment of Peter the Great – the most active of all Russian westernists, whose influence on Russia's development the slavophiles deplored. They attached importance

The execution of the assassins of Alexander II on 3 April 1881
in Semyonovsky Square, St Petersburg. They wore the black clothes prescribed for
condemned criminals; the placards round their necks say 'Tsaricide'. For the actual
hanging they were robed in white, hooded shrouds. Sophia Perovsky, in the centre,
was the first woman to be executed in Russia. The men were Andrew Zhelyabov,
Nicholas Kibalchich, Timothy Mikhaylov and Nicholas Rysakov.

to the village commune as a traditional Slav institution, to the
Orthodox Church, to the collection of folk-lore material – in fact
to everything covered by the charismatic and untranslatable word
narodny (popular, national, folksy, essentially Russian) from which
narodnik ('populist') derives. Gogol and Dostoyevsky may be
regarded as slavophiles, and another important writer associated
with the movement was S. T. Aksakov, whose sons Konstantin and
Ivan became important theorists of slavophilism. The slavophile
movement lost impetus in the 1860s.

The forties and sixties

The 1840s had been an age of intellectual ferment of a more
philosophical kind than were the concerns of many political
oppositionists from the 1860s onwards. It was the interpretation of
German and French philosophers and social thinkers, rather than
the manufacture of bombs, that interested the men of the forties.
They had more use too for the arts, for it was an outstanding
feature of the nihilist generation to judge art solely from the point
of view of utility – witness the nihilist cliché to the effect that a
good pair of boots was more valuable than the entire works of
Pushkin. There is thus a marked contrast between oppositionists
of the two generations – the older one being polite, philosophical
and emotional (see Herzen's long accounts of his love affairs and
sentimental friendships), while the younger one was brusque,
down-to-earth and more concerned with revolutionary action.
The first was the age of circles and discussion groups, the second
of conspiracies. To some extent it is a contrast between patrician
and plebeian, between talk and action, and in literature between
Turgenev's *Fathers and Children* in his novel with that title.

The intelligentsia

The term intelligentsia originated in Russia, where (by contrast
with its use in the present-day Soviet Union and as applied to

other countries) it generally referred only to 'that part of educated society which held radical left-wing views' (Utechin, *Dictionary*, p. 235). Thus a leading intellectual such as Dostoyevsky cannot properly be called a member of the Russian intelligentsia, since he was a militant conservative, at least in later life. He would not himself have wished to be regarded as an *intelligent* (the Russian word for a member of the intelligentsia) – in fact he lost few opportunities to denounce the intelligentsia. His view is not on the whole shared by students of the period, who have been inclined to praise *intelligenty* for their courage and high-mindedness, but he was not alone among the better-known Russian writers in taking a jaundiced view.

Chekhov too had moods of impatience with the Russian intelligentsia, which he once described as 'hypocritical, false, hysterical, uneducated and lazy' (letter of 22nd February 1899). But his views on the Russian intelligentsia were not consistent – and indeed it would be absurd to look for consistency in his casual asides on the subject. On balance he shows himself as an advocate of the intelligentsia, while distrusting those representatives of it who were most extreme in their political views. Whether through personal distaste or censorship conditions, he is rarely found portraying a significant type of his age – the Russian revolutionary – though he did so in somewhat muted form in his *Anonymous Story*. One point which struck him was the extreme intolerance of Russian political oppositionists. 'Under the flag of science, art and persecuted freedom of thought', he once claimed, Russia would one day be ruled by 'toads and crocodiles the like of which were unknown even in Spain at the time of the Inquisition' (letter of 27th August 1888).

Revolutionaries and nihilists

Through the history of Russian nineteenth- and twentieth-century revolutionaries two themes run in counterpoint. First there is action, which sounds as if it might come from some bizarre thriller,

ncluding such episodes as burrowing tunnels under roads and
railways over which the Tsar might be expected to pass; the shooting, stabbing and bombing of police officials, ministers, governor-
generals and grand dukes; daring robberies ('expropriations')
conducted to provide revolutionary funds; secret printing presses;
pamphlets calling on the peasantry to massacre the landlords;
penetration of revolutionary cells by police spies and counter-
penetration of the police by revolutionary spies; and all the rest of
the colourful paraphernalia of disguise, dissimulation and conspiratorial terrorism. Hysteria, courage, treachery, obstinacy,
recklessness and self-sacrifice are all amply illustrated in the history
of Russian revolution.

Alongside all this went the theoretical argument. What was the
role of the peasantry to be in the coming revolution? Or of the
urban proletariat? Must Russia pass through the stage of capitalism like the advanced countries of western Europe? Or could she
take her own path and found socialism on such traditional institutions as the village commune and the artels (workers associations)?
Was murdering the Tsar such a good idea after all? These and
kindred topics were endlessly canvassed, some in plain or disguised
form in the pages of the press, others in illegal pamphlets or
conspiratorial meetings. According to temperament, individuals
dabbled in ink or dynamite, and many were adept with both.

No comprehensive description of the theory or practice of
Russian revolution need be attempted in the present study. This
is partly because full and excellent accounts already exist, and
partly because censorship made it impossible for writers to
illustrate the revolutionary struggle frankly and openly in imaginative literature, where it does nevertheless play a certain role.

An important fictional study of Russian revolutionaries is that
found in Dostoyevsky's novel *Devils*. As an enthusiastic supporter
of the autocracy, Dostoyevsky was less hampered by censorship
than were other authors more sympathetic to political opposition.
His study is, accordingly, not at all a balanced picture of the
Russian political situation, but a ferociously intemperate denuncia-

tion of the Russian revolutionary movement. It was, however, based on some knowledge of the facts. Dostoyevsky's arch-villain, Peter Verkhovensky, is modelled on a grotesque and violent figure from real life, the revolutionary conspirator Sergey Nechayev. Dostoyevsky even used Nechayev's name for his villain in the draft notes which he made for the novel. The main episode of *Devils*, the murder of Shatov, is based on the actual murder of the student Ivanov, organised by Nechayev on 21st November 1869 in order to bind his fellow-conspirators together in common guilt. The emphasis on deception, including the pretence of controlling a vast and largely imaginary organisation of secret cells, is also taken from Nechayev's biography. Nechayev himself escaped to Switzerland after Ivanov's murder, but was extradited to Russia and confined in the fortress of St Peter and St Paul in St Petersburg. Here he won over some of his guards, and in early 1881 even managed to correspond from his cell with members of the People's Will group at the time when they were just about to assassinate Alexander II. Nechayev died in the fortress dungeons in 1883.

Devils describes the moral disintegration of an unnamed provincial town, brought about by the nihilists of whom Peter Verkhovensky is the leader. The concept of nihilism is an elusive one and the word has no exact and generally accepted meaning – and yet it describes an important social phenomenon of the mid-nineteenth century, more especially of the 1860s. It is one of those unfortunate terms which are both descriptive and abusive. Dostoyevsky himself tended to apply it to all those whose political views were to the left of his own – a fair slice, one is tempted to say, of the human race. He was also fond of the pejorative derivative *nigilyatina* ('nihilist carrion').

The features of a typical nihilist were: being a student; wearing unconventional dress; long hair (for men), short hair (for girls); the preaching and practice of free love; devotion to the rights of women; also, on the theoretical side, materialism, utilitarianism, atheism and a belief in science and human welfare. Anyone exhibiting a significant number of the above indicators was liable to be dismissed as a nihilist by people who disliked him, in addition to which the word was often used as a vague synonym for any sort of revolutionary. As the above description shows, it is not quite fair to accuse nihilists of believing in nothing (*nihil*). Even if Pisarev, who is considered the main real-life nihilist, did once put forward the much-quoted axiom that 'whatever can be smashed must be smashed', he did at least add: 'Whatever survives a blow has value'.

Pisarev further complicates the picture because, unlike most nihilists, he was prepared to accept this abusive name as applying to those who shared his views, though he preferred the term 'realist'. The name nihilist itself was, incidentally, first popularised in Turgenev's novel *Fathers and Children* – after *Devils* the most important fictional study of the type. Here Turgenev attempted to give a sympathetic picture of the nihilist in his hero Bazarov, who is, however, chiefly memorable for his general rudeness or brusqueness, certainly a common nihilist characteristic, rather than for any attractive positive qualities.

Another important Russian novel to treat the phenomenon is in effect an apologia for nihilism. This is Chernyshevsky's *What is to be done?* (1863), written in prison. The novel became the bible of politically disaffected young Russians, though its merits as a work of literature are modest. In fact it now reads as an unintentionally comic work, if one can forget the circumstances in which it was written and the harsh fate suffered by its author, whose life makes a more gripping story than his fiction. A heroic, bespectacled figure of inflexible will and unshakable opposition to the autocracy, he became a martyr to imprisonment and exile. Before being dispatched to Siberia he was made to take part in the ludicrous ceremony of public disgrace, called civil execution, in St Petersburg. Here he had a sword ceremonially broken over his head, after being conveyed to a 'pillar of shame' on a scaffold especially erected in the Mytny Square. According to one eye-witness account, he spent the time while the sentence was being read spitting with 'more than nonchalance' (Gernet, ii, p. 279). This

form of public disgrace was sometimes inflicted on revolutionaries as a prelude to imprisonment and exile.

Populists

Herzen was at one time an all-out westernist, but after emigrating in 1847 found his enthusiasm cooled by exposure to western Europe as it was and not as he had imagined it. He came to agree with the slavophiles on the importance of the Russian village commune, though to him its value was that it seemed to offer Russia the prospect of a short cut to socialism. The link thus established between westernism and slavophilism makes Herzen the originator of Russian populism.

Populism arose in the 1870s when – as later – it was notable for two contrasting modes of activity. The first of these was peaceful, the so-called 'movement to the people', which took place in 1873–4 when hundreds or thousands of young men and women went to the Russian villages to influence the peasantry and thus solve the basic crux among Russian revolutionary problems: how

to make contact with the inarticulate elements among the forces
of disintegration, the peasant masses. This attempt was a failure
and led to the arrest and trial of many who took part – the episode
forms a theme in Turgenev's last novel, *Virgin Soil*. In 1877 the
populists formed a secret political party called Land and Freedom,
thus reviving a name used by an earlier clandestine revolutionary
group in the 1860s. But they could not agree over the crucial issue
of violence, and in 1879 split into two factions, reformist and
terrorist. Members of the former adopted the name Black Repartition, and wished to promote agrarian reform through land
redistribution. Not believing in political solutions, they were
opposed to terrorism as a political weapon. The other faction,
which did practise terrorism, was People's Will, and included the
serf's son Zhelyabov and his mistress the provincial governor's
daughter Sophia Perovsky. They made attempt after attempt on
the life of Alexander II, culminating in the successful assassination
by the Yekaterininsky Canal on March 1st 1881.

The accession of a tough-minded monarch in Alexander III, and
the rigorous measures taken against the revolutionary movement
during his reign, led to a slump in populism as expressed in
violence. Thus the unsuccessful attempt to assassinate the Tsar in
1887 by Lenin's elder brother Alexander Ulyanov, among others,
was out of character with the general tenor of the 1880s, when
oppositionists followed a more modest policy, sometimes termed
that 'of little deeds'. The fashion was now to abandon the hope of
revolutionary upheaval for the time being and to concentrate on
helping and getting to know the peasant, for example by working
as a doctor or teacher for one of the zemstvos. The populists
operated both illegally and legally. They published openly, their
two main journals being *Notes of the Fatherland* and *Russian
Wealth* (St Petersburg, 1880–1918). The main influence on these
two publications was the leading theoretician of the movement,
N. K. Mikhaylovsky. Another important populist leader was P. L.
Lavrov, author of the influential *Historical Letters* (1870), who was
active mainly as an *émigré*.

The populist point of view was expressed by a number of novelists of peasant life, including two minor figures, N. N. Zlatovratsky and P. V. Zasodimsky, who followed the tradition of idealising rural Russia. A more balanced view of the village is found in the work of another populist, Ertel, whose long novel *The Gardenins* (1889) is a major work in Russian peasant fiction. Another writer associated with the movement is Gleb Uspensky, who became disillusioned with populism and left some especially sour pictures of peasant conditions in his *Power of the Soil* (1882). Korolenko too was associated with populism, and was in general one of the most important and determined oppositionists among Russian authors both as a journalist and as an imaginative writer. He tried to arouse sympathy for oppressed national minorities, as in one of his best-known stories, *Makar's Dream*, and attacked the abuses committed by the imperial police and law-courts. His sketch *A Strange Girl* (1880) contains a description of a young revolutionary.

Social revolutionaries

Populism rallied towards the end of the century under the reign of a new and relatively weak-willed Tsar, Nicholas II. In 1902 a new underground party, that of the Socialist Revolutionaries, was formed. It was basically a peasant-orientated movement, placing its faith, according to populist tradition, in the village commune. One aim of the party was to socialise land and give it to the peasantry, with periodical redistributions as necessary and without compensation to the landowners. But the most spectacular feature of Socialist Revolutionary policy was the maintenance of the old People's Will tactic of practising political assassination.

Marxists

Political assassination was one of the points on which the Socialist Revolutionaries were challenged by the Russian marxist movement, which rejected political terror from a belief that it did not produce results, and certainly not out of sentiment or squeamishness. The main point of contention between Socialist Revolutionaries and marxists concerned the peasants. Marxists regarded the peasantry as a backward force, inferior in revolutionary potential to the urban proletariat, and it was their habit to use a formula calculated to set any Socialist Revolutionary's teeth on edge: 'the idiocy of rural life'.

Marxists also disagreed with populism in believing that Russia was not to follow a special historical evolution of its own, but should pass through the phase of capitalism just like any ordinary western European state that lacked the advantages, which to marxists were of dubious importance, of Russian corporate institutions. As already stated, Russian was the first foreign language into which Marx's *Capital* was translated. G. V. Plekhanov, the main founder of Russian marxism, had been a leading theorist in the Land and Freedom movement between 1876 and 1879. When, in the latter year, the movement split into a reformist and terrorist wing, he headed the former, but shortly after emigrating in 1880 broke with populism and became a convinced marxist, founding a marxist group abroad called the Liberation of Labour.

In the 1880s illegal marxist groups were meeting in Russia. The Russian Social Democratic Labour Party, founded secretly in 1898, brought them together and was the direct forerunner of the present Communist Party of the Soviet Union. Its early history includes the ascendancy acquired by Lenin and the split into the two factions of Bolshevik and Menshevik in 1903. Russian marxists were to prove most effective on the conspiratorial level, but did have their 'legal' activities as well, and were able for instance to publish the magazine *Life* in which some of Gorky's work appeared.

Gorky became the most celebrated writer to support Bolshevism, but had been in trouble with the imperial police long before the Social Democratic Party was founded. After being arrested in 1888 for associating with a subversive group, he was under constant police supervision. Other episodes in his career include being expelled from Nizhny Novgorod in 1901, and – in the following year – having his election as an honorary member of the imperial Academy of Sciences annulled at the personal initiative of Nicholas II. (The episode led Chekhov and Korolenko to resign their own honorary membership of the Academy out of sympathy with Gorky.) In 1905 Gorky increased his revolutionary qualifications by being briefly imprisoned in the fortress of St Peter and St Paul and by meeting Lenin for the first time.

Dazzled by the terrorist tactics of the Socialist Revolutionaries, the imperial authorities had been slow to discern danger from Russia's marxists, who at first seemed dull, doctrinaire creatures bogged down in economic abstractions and less apt with dynamite and pistol than the picturesque heirs of People's Will. But before long the authorities did find that they had to take their marxists more seriously.

Tolstoy and the opposition

Though revolutionary activity could not be adequately reflected in contemporary literature, one work containing detailed portraits of revolutionaries is Tolstoy's *Resurrection*. Here Catherine Maslov's companions in prison and exile provide the opportunity for a number of revolutionary studies. For instance, some features in the revolutionary Marya Shchetin are based on a real-life prototype, N. A. Armfeld. In the same novel Nekhlyudov's attempts to intercede for imprisoned revolutionaries include an interview with a certain 'Baron Kriegsmuth', the real-life Baron Von Maydel, Commandant of the fortress of St Peter and St Paul, which Tolstoy himself visited and where hundreds of revolutionaries were held in the course of the century. The relaxation, amounting almost to abolition, of censorship after the 1905 Revolution, made more outspoken studies of the phenomenon possible in such works as Gorky's *Mother*. Two notable stories by Leonid Andreyev, *The Governor* (1906) and *Seven Who Were Hanged* (1908), are based on the theme of political assassination.

If it should be asked which individual among the great Russian writers contributed most to the disintegration of the monarchy and of imperial society, the answer must surely be Tolstoy himself. He rejected violence and was more a pacifist–anarchist than a revolutionary. But he battered away with persistent eloquence against most of the traditional allegiances of the Russian Empire, as against the trappings of modern civilisation in general. Should the imperial Russian citizen pay his taxes, defend his country, respect its law-courts and its social structure? Should he even sleep with his wife? To all these questions Tolstoy answered a resounding and impressively reasoned 'no'. His powerful arguments, widely circulated both legally and in clandestine copies, had an influence which is hard to assess, but must have been great. If he toppled no bastions, he certainly helped to pry them loose.

Not all the many features of Russian society rejected by Tolstoy can be accepted as unmitigated evils. Among them was, after all, Russian literature itself – and indeed the world's art as a whole. Much of this – including the works of Shakespeare, Homer and Wagner, as well as his own early writings – was attacked by Tolstoy in critical studies of which the most important is *What is Art?* (1897). The world has not accepted Tolstoy's verdict on aesthetic matters – or on very much else either – and though imperial Russia is often to be condemned in its political and social aspects, Russian nineteenth-century literature remains unchallenged as one of the Empire's abiding achievements.

Select bibliography

Sections 1 to 3 contain works written in or available in English, which may be found suitable for further reading. Works of Russian imaginative literature are not included, but useful information about translations of these into English can be obtained from the notes to the two books by Marc Slonim included in Section 1. These also include references to bibliographies of translations into English of leading Russian writers, and of works in English about them.

Section 4 is simply a list of other works, whether in English or not, to which reference happens to be made in the text or which have been found particularly useful. Though this section contains much interesting material, it is not intended as a systematic list for recommended reading, many of the works concerned being specialised or not easily accessible. Nor is this section offered as a comprehensive indication of source material.

An asterisk is occasionally used when more than one edition of a work is mentioned to indicate the edition to which reference has been made in the text.

1 Works on nineteenth century Russian literature and authors

Freeborn, Richard, *Turgenev: the Novelist's Novelist*, Oxford, 1960.

Harkins, William E., *Dictionary of Russian Literature*, New York, 1956; London, 1957.

Hingley, Ronald, *Chekhov: a Biographical and Critical Study*, London, 1950. *The Undiscovered Dostoyevsky*, London, 1962.

Magarshack, David, *Chekhov: a Life*, London, 1952. *Turgenev: a Life*, London, 1954. *Gogol: a Life*, London, 1957. *Dostoevsky*, London, 1962.

Maude, Aylmer, *The Life of Tolstoy: First Fifty Years* and *Later Years*, first published 1908; rewritten and revised, London, 1930 (2 vols).

Mirsky, D.S., *A History of Russian Literature*, ed. and abridged by Francis J. Whitfield (London, 1949*); this is a combined and abridged version of Mirsky's *Contemporary Russian Literature, 1881–1925*, London, 1926 and *History of Russian Literature from Earliest Times to the Death of Dostoevsky (1881)*, London, 1927.

Simmons, Ernest J., *Pushkin*, Cambridge, Mass. and London, 1937. *Leo Tolstoy*, Boston, 1946; London, 1949. *Dostoyevsky: the Making of a Novelist*, New York and London, 1950 and 1963. *Chekhov: a Biography*, Boston, 1962; London, 1963.

Slonim, Marc, *The Epic of Russian Literature: from its Origins through Tolstoy*, New York, 1950. *Modern Russian Literature: from Chekhov to the Present*, New York, 1953.

Yarmolinsky, Avrahm, *Dostoevsky: his Life and Art*, New York and London, 1957. *Turgenev: the Man, his Art, and his Age*, New York and London, 1959.

2 General histories of Russia

Clarkson, Jesse D., *A History of Russia from the Ninth Century*, New York, 1961.

Florinsky, Michael T., *Russia: a History and an Interpretation*, New York, 1953 (2 vols).

Karpovich, Michael, *Imperial Russia, 1801–1917*, New York, 1932.

Kornilov, A.A., *Modern Russian History*, tr. A.S.Kaun, New York, 1943.

Pares, B., *A History of Russia*, 2nd ed., New York, 1928.

Platonov, S.F., *History of Russia*, tr. E.Aronsberg, New York, 1925.

Riasanovsky, Nicholas V., *A History of Russia*, New York, 1963.

Sumner, B.H., *Survey of Russian History*, London, 1944.

Vernadsky, George, *A History of Russia*, 4th, revised ed., New Haven, 1954; first published, 1929.

See also: Shapiro, David, *A Select Bibliography of Works in English on Russian History, 1801–1917*, Oxford, 1962.

3 Studies of aspects of the problem

Allen, W.E.D., *History of the Georgian People*, London, 1932. *The Ukraine: a History*, Cambridge, 1950.

Billington, James H., *Mikhailovsky and Russian Populism*, Oxford, 1958.

Blum, Jerome, *Lord and Peasant in Russia from the Ninth to the Nineteenth Century*, Princeton, 1961; New York, 1964*.

Bruford, W.H., *Chekhov and his Russia: a Sociological Study*, London, 1948.

Carr, Edward Hallett, *The Romantic Exiles: a Nineteenth Century Portrait Gallery*, London, 1933. *Michael Bakunin*, London, 1937.

Conybeare, Frederick C., *Russian Dissenters*, Cambridge, Mass., 1921.

Curtiss, John Sheldon, *Church and State in Russia: the Last Years of the Empire, 1900–1917*, New York, 1940.

Footman, David, *Red Prelude: a Life of A.I.Zhelyabov*, London, 1944.

Greenberg, Louis, *The Jews in Russia*, New Haven, 1944–51 (2 vols.): vol. i, *The Struggle for Emancipation;* vol. ii, *The Struggle for Emancipation, 1881–1917*.

Hare, Richard, *Pioneers of Russian Social Thought*, London, 1951.

250

Herzen, Alexander, *My Past and Thoughts*, tr. Constance Garnett, London, 1924–7 (6 vols).

Kennan, George, *Siberia and the Exile System*, New York, 1891 (2 vols).

Kochan, Lionel, *The Making of Modern Russia*, London, 1962.

Lampert, E., *Studies in Rebellion*, London, 1957. *Sons against Fathers: Studies in Russian Radicalism and Revolution*, Oxford, 1965.

Leroy-Beaulieu, A., *The Empire of the Tsars and the Russians*, tr. Z. Ragozine, New York, 1893–6, [a translation of *L'Empire des Tsars et les Russes*, Paris, 1881–9*] (3 vols).

Mackenzie Wallace, D., *Russia*, London, 1877*; also later edition, London, 1912 (2 vols).

Malia, Martin E., *Alexander Herzen and the Birth of Russian Socialism*, Cambridge, Mass., 1961.

Masaryk, T.G., *The Spirit of Russia*, tr. E. and C. Paul, with additional chapters by J. Slavik, London, 1955 (2 vols).

Mavor, James, *An Economic History of Russia*, 2nd ed., London, 1925 (2 vols).

Miliukov, Paul, *Outlines of Russian Culture*, ed. Michael Karpovich, Part I: *Religion and the Church;* Part II: *Literature;* Part III: *Architecture, Painting and Music*, Philadelphia, 1942.

Monas, Sidney, *The Third Section: Police and Society in Russia under Nicholas I*, Cambridge, Mass., 1961.

Mosse, W.E., *Alexander II and the Modernization of Russia*, London, 1958.

Riasanovsky, Nicholas V., *Nicholas I and Official Nationality in Russia, 1825–1855*, Berkeley and Los Angeles, 1959.

Robinson, Geroid T., *Rural Russia under the Old Régime*, 2nd printing, New York, 1949.

Semyonov, Yuri, *Siberia: its Conquest and Development*, tr. J.R. Foster, London, 1963.

Seton-Watson, Hugh, *The Decline of Imperial Russia, 1855–1914*, London, 1952.

Stepniak (S.M. Kravchinsky), *Underground Russia*, 2nd ed., London, 1883. *The Russian Peasantry: their Agrarian Condition, Social Life and Religion*, new ed., New York, 1905.

Troyat, Henri, *Daily Life in Russia under the Last Tsar*, tr. Malcolm Barnes, London, 1961.

Utechin, S.V., *Everyman's Concise Encyclopaedia of Russia*, London, 1961. *Russian Political Thought: a Concise History*, New York, 1964.

Venturi, Franco, *Roots of Revolution*, tr. Francis Haskell, London, 1959.
Westwood, J.N., *A History of Russian Railways*, London, 1964.

4 Other works

Aleksandrov, V.A. and others, ed., *Narody yevropeyskoy chasti SSSR* [The peoples of the European part of the U.S.S.R.], Moscow, 1964.

Baedeker, Karl, *Russland, nebst Teheran, Port Arthur, Peking* [Russia with Port Arthur, Teheran and Pekin], 7th ed., Leipzig, 1912.

Burnaby, Fred., *A Ride to Khiva: Travels and Adventures in Central Asia*, London, 1876.

Christian, R.F., *Tolstoy's 'War and Peace'*, Oxford, 1962.

Edwards, Sutherland, *Russians at Home: Unpolitical Sketches*, London, 1861.

Gernet, M.N., *Istoriya tsarskoy tyurmy* [History of the Tsarist prison], 2nd ed., Moscow, 1951* (3 vols); also 3rd ed., Moscow, 1960–4 (5 vols).

Hingley, Ronald, ed., *Chekhov, the Oxford*, vol. iii, London, 1964; vol. viii, London, 1965.

Isayev, Andrey, '*Velikorusskiye plemena Moskovskoy oblasti*' [The Great Russians of the Moscow Region] in: *Zhivopisnaya Rossiya* [Picturesque Russia], ed. P.P.Semyonov, vol. vi, part ii, St. Petersburg, 1898.

Kolarz, Walter, *Religion in the Soviet Union*, London, 1961.

Kjellberg, Lennart, *Den klassiska romanens Ryssland* [Russia of the classical novel], Stockholm, 1964.

Kovalevsky, V.I., ed., *Rossiya v kontse XIX veka* [Russia at the end of the nineteenth century], St Petersburg, 1900*; tr. into French as *La Russie à la fin du XIX siècle*, Paris, 1900.

Pushkin, A.S., *Eugene Onegin: a Novel in Verse*, ed., tr. and commentary by V. Nabokov, New York and London, 1964 (4 vols).

Rozenberg, Vl. and Yakushkin, V., *Russkaya pechat i tsenzura v proshlom i nastoyashchem* [The Russian press and censorship, past and present], Moscow, 1905.

Schlesinger, M. L., *Land und Leute in Russland* [Land and people in Russia], 2nd ed., Berlin, 1909.

Turgenev, I.S., *Sobraniye sochineny* [Collected works], Moscow, 1954 (12 vols).

Vinogradov, V.V., and others, ed., *Chekhov, Literaturnoye nasledstvo:* [Literary heritage: Chekhov], Moscow, 1960.

Woolf, Virginia, 'The Russian Point of View' in *The Common Reader*, First Series, London, 1938.

Acknowledgments

Warmest thanks are due to four colleagues: Dr S. V. Utechin, who kindly read the draft manuscript, and whose advice and help have been keenly appreciated; to Mr J. S. G. Simmons for his most valuable advice on bibliography; to Dr A. J. Krailsheimer; to Dr George Katkov; also to my wife for her constant help and encouragement; and to the Oxford University Press for permitting me to reprint material on pp. 170-2 and 189 from my translations of Chekhov in *The Oxford Chekhov*, vol. viii. Acknowledgment is due to the following for the illustrations (the number refers to the page on which the picture appears): frontispiece, 12, 14, 16, 17, 19, 22, 25, 26, 30, 35, 37, 152, 167, 171, 173, 178, 187, 188, 206 (left), 211, 212, 222 SCR Photo Library; 11, 29, 45, 48, 61, 109, 116, 117 (bottom), 146, 150, 180, 181, 203 (left), 206 (right), 242 Novosti Press Agency; 39, 68, 69, 72, 78, 79, 80, 81, 84, 96, 100, 105, 114, 117 (top), 126–7, 136, 147, 153, 159, 164, 168, 169, 202, 232 John R. Freeman; 40, 58–9, 177 Snark International; 52, 183, 203 (right) Radio Times Hulton Picture Library; 60 Collection of the Library of Congress; 98, 99, 107, 236 Mansell Collection; 161 Recklinghausen Ikon Museum. The maps were drawn by A.W. Gatrell & Co. Ltd.

R. H.

Index

253